EXCAVATING KIRJATH-SEPHER'S TEN CITIES

This is a volume in the Arno Press collection

AMERICA
AND
THE HOLY LAND

Advisory Editor
Professor Moshe Davis

Editorial Board
Professor Robert Theodore Handy
Professor Jules Davids
Dr. Nathan M. Kaganoff

See last pages of this volume for a complete list of titles.

EXCAVATING KIRJATH-SEPHER'S
TEN CITIES

MELVIN GROVE KYLE

ARNO PRESS

A New York Times Company

New York / 1977

Editorial Supervision: JOSEPH CELLINI

———◆———

Reprint Edition 1977 by Arno Press Inc.

AMERICA AND THE HOLY LAND
ISBN for complete set: 0-405-10220-8
See last pages of this volume for titles.

Manufactured in the United States of America

———◆———

Library of Congress Cataloging in Publication Data

Kyle, Melvin Grove, 1858-1933.
    Excavating Kirjath-Sepher's ten cities.

    (America and the Holy Land)
    Reprint of the ed. published by Eerdmans,
Grand Rapids, in series: The James Sprunt lectures,
1932.
    1. Tell Beit Mirsim, Palestine. 2. Bible.
O. T.--Antiquities. 3. Palestine--Antiquities.
4. Kyle, Melvin Grove, 1858-1933. I. Title.
II. Series. III. Series: The James Sprunt
lectures ; 1932.
DS110.T393K94 1977   221.9'3   77-70714
ISBN 0-405-10262-3

In tribute to
DANIEL G. ROSS
for his leadership, friendship and counsel

EXCAVATING KIRJATH-SEPHER'S TEN CITIES

A Palestine Fortress from Abraham's Day to Nebuchadnezzar's

BOOKS BY *MELVIN GROVE KYLE*

BIBLIOTHECA SACRA COMPANY
  Deciding Voice of the Monuments
  Moses and the Monuments
  Problem of the Pentateuch

FLEMING H. REVELL COMPANY
  Explorations at Sodom
  Mooring Masts of Revelation

WM. B. EERDMANS PUBLISHING COMPANY
  Excavating Kirjath-sepher's Ten Cities

MELVIN GROVE KYLE, D.D., LL.D.

EXCAVATING KIRJATH-SEPHER'S TEN CITIES

A Palestine Fortress from Abraham's Day to Nebuchadnezzar's

THE CULTURE OF BIBLE LANDS, THE MATRIX OF BIBLE NARRATIVES

The James Sprunt Lectures

1932

Union Theological Seminary
Richmond, Va.

BY

MELVIN GROVE KYLE, D.D., LL.D.

Research Lecturer
Pittsburgh-Xenia Seminary
and
Permanent Lecturer on Archaeology
Louisville Presbyterian Seminary
and
Dallas Evangelical Theological College

Wm. B. EERDMANS PUBLISHING COMPANY
Grand Rapids, Michigan
1934

THE JAMES SPRUNT LECTURES

In 1911 Mr. James Sprunt of Wilmington, North Carolina, established a perpetual lectureship at Union Theological Seminary, Richmond, Virginia, which would enable the institution to secure from time to time the services of distinguished ministers and authoritative scholars as special lecturers on subjects connected with various departments of Christian thought and Christian work. The lecturers are chosen by the Faculty of the Seminary and a committee of the Board of Trustees, and lectures are published after their delivery in accordance with a contract between the lecturer and these representatives of the institution. The series of lectures on this foundation for the year 1932 is presented in this volume.

To

WILLIAM F. ALBRIGHT,

Scholar, Colleague, Friend

FOREWORD

THE materials which enter into this book, together with much in addition, have appeared from time to time during the past seven years in the *Sunday School Times, Bibliotheca Sacra,* and briefly in sundry other publications; they are here re-arranged and presented as a connected story and illustrated by many original photographs.

No man does such a work unaided. It is a pleasure here to make special acknowledgment of my indebtedness to the generosity of Pittsburgh-Xenia Seminary, the Seventh United Presbyterian Church of Frankford, Philadelphia, the American School of Oriental Research in Jerusalem, the Department of Antiquities of the Palestine Government, and to a few personal friends who have helped to make the work possible.

Then also to life long friends, the American Colony, my Jerusalem home for forty years, to the fellowship of the genial scholars of the world in this field of endeavor, and most of all to the loving care of Providence in one hundred and fifty thousand miles of travel on sea and land through fire and shipwreck and storm and war.

I am also indebted to the Howard-Severance Company for their permission to use the cut on "Comparative View of Types of Pottery," which is reproduced from their copyright work, the *"International Standard Bible Encyclopaedia."*   M. G. K.

DR. M. G. KYLE'S manuscript of this book was undergoing final revision at the time of his death. The work was completed by his close associate, Dr. J. L. Kelso of the Pittsburgh-Xenia Seminary. Most of the illustrations used in the book are from the collection of Dr. M. G. Kyle or are graciously furnished by various members of the staffs at *Tell Beit Mirsim.*   J. L. K.

CONTENTS

LIST OF ILLUSTRATIONS

INTRODUCTION

A STORY that enables people to see the progress of a
work must be a record of that progress and written at
the place during the progress. Realism is as valuable in a
story of work as in a story of life. So this narrative comes
directly from Camp *Tell Beit Mirsim* during the progress of
the work in the various campaigns described; the material
was actually so prepared. The results will thus grow into
completeness in the thought of the reader exactly as they
did in the experience of the archæologists.

It also seems to me that any story worth telling, is worth
telling in a way to be fully understood by the public for
whom it is intended, who are yet unfamiliar with the technicalities of the story. So, while the work was a most
strictly scientific work and the account will bear the test at
every point, I will endeavor to tell the story in popular
language as nearly devoid of technical terminology as
possible, and never to permit myself to become so engrossed
in abstractions as to lose touch with immediate life round
about the work and round about the world of the reader.
For this ancient history is not to be a thing apart; it is part
and parcel of life. People of ancient days were of the
same human race as ourselves, facing the same problems of
life and the same perplexities, and with equivalent natural
equipment.

The various staffs of the different campaigns will be introduced at the appropriate places in the narrative: I would
bear cordial testimony here to the ever willing helpfulness
of those scholars, and especially to my distinguished colleague, Dr. Albright, Director of the American School of
Oriental Research in Jerusalem, now also the head of the
Department of Semitic Philology of Johns Hopkins University. His influence is never wanting at any part of this
story. His marvelous breadth of knowledge was with us at
every point as a check against mistakes, and I wish the
sweet spirit of his never failing courtesy may pervade the
narrative as it did every part of the work.

The work will be described in the order both of discovery

15

and of the ages of culture. In order to keep the discoveries clearly in the order of the ages, it occasionally became necessary to transfer the account of a discovery from one campaign to another.

Many years ago from the desert of Sinai, I wrote as follows:[1] "A somewhat hazy, precarious clause in a bargain with the Towarah Bedouin for the convoy of a party to Sinai had been that they would give the travelers a glimpse of the turquoise mines. So they peered under great rocks and into crevices where real gems could be found, and enjoyed in sober-mindedness the thrill of expectation which the romance of childhood with its dreams of gold mines had awakened. But the greatest marvel of that day was to find the gems not in crevices or peeping out of dust and rubbish, or like nuts in a shell rolling about with the appearance of worthless pebbles, but embedded in the very heart of the solid rock, where blind but patient industry discovered them by breaking them out of the bed in which they have lain from the foundation of the world.

Now if one of those dusky miners should exhibit a large, rare gem of marked peculiarities of shape, with the claim that it had come from that mine, and we should find the empty matrix in a rock into which every nicety of the gem fitted exactly, or if we found a strange hole in the rock and the miner should produce a gem which exactly fitted it and say: 'I found it there,' we would not be able to resist the conclusion that the miner's story was true." In like manner the culture of Bible lands is the matrix of Bible narratives; the way they fit the matrix is the conclusive test of the correctness of the narratives.

Now to the telling of the story of Kirjath-sepher and the unfolding of that Culture of Bible Lands which is the Matrix of Bible Narratives.

---

[1] KYLE, *Deciding Voice of the Monuments*, p. 158. edition of 1924.

PART I

CAMPAIGN OF 1926

CHAPTER I

TO "BOOK-TOWN"

Camp *Tell Beit Mirsim.*

PLANS in the Orient move slowly. We may not be unmindful of the tragic fate of the man who "tried to hustle the East." So, patience! For instance, a telegram of greeting and good news from my colleague, Dr. Albright, Director of the American School of Oriental Research in Jerusalem, was actually delivered to me in Jerusalem after I had seen Dr. Albright and received his greetings in person. Such is life here. The telegram itself was informing and cheering, though belated in delivery. It read, "Expecting you — excavation permit granted — negotiations begun." This meant that unrestricted permission for excavation of the whole site chosen had been given by the Department of Antiquities of the Palestine government, and that negotiations with the owners of the land were under way.

The site had been visited by Dr. C. S. Fisher, the distinguished American archæologist, and most enthusiastically approved by him as one of the most promising *tells* for excavation in all Palestine. It is small, compact, with walls clearly showing nearly all the way around, and remains of structures actually sticking out of the ground, inviting examination, and the gateway conspicuously standing out to welcome investigators. This is most encouraging at the outset, as it assures us some immediate results without having to wait until mountains of debris are removed.

While I tarry in Jerusalem until time to start to Kirjath-sepher, I am deep in archæological lore at the Museums of the American and British Schools, making a rather intense study of the pottery of Palestine. "Well, of all things dry and dusty!" someone will say. To the average reader of Biblical things, the patter about old potsherds is to the last degree wearisome, and mysterious besides. But when one perceives the significance of these plebeian relics of bygone

19

civilization, such old fragments become most fascinating. History is written on them and told by them.

I wonder if I can so illustrate that idea as to illuminate it. A good many years ago I had the pleasure of visiting *Huis ten Bosch,* the Palace in the Woods, at the Hague, Holland. It is a quaint and exquisite old palace full of treasures, a veritable museum that displays some very interesting history of a comparatively modern world. Among the treasures there displayed are the richest and most remarkable Chinese fabrics and bric-a-brac. Why these? They were presented to the Dutch traders on their early visits to the closed Celestial Empire. They signalize the beginning of the Dutch far-eastern trade. Chinese things are now so familiar in the eyes of the Occidental world that they excite no comment, but *these mark the historical period* when Chinese things were first brought to the Western world and were followed by the development of the great China industry of modern Europe and America. The presence of these things at the Hague is to mark thus an epoch in history.

So it is here in this museum at Jerusalem in two little cases among a number of others. In these cases are not delicate, fragile Chinese cups and saucers, but, instead, rather coarse, but useful articles of Palestinian ware of the Late Bronze Age from about 1600 B. C. onward for some centuries. These are in one case. In another case along-side of this is arranged another collection of articles which, piece by piece, correspond in materials and design and coloring to these pieces of Palestine. This latter collection is entirely from Cyprus and Crete and represents the Cypro-Phœnician civilization. These Palestinian things which belong just before the time of the Conquest, are thus entirely Cypriote in design and materials. The Cypriote articles show whence the Palestinian pottery was derived. They represent a historical invasion of Palestine at a time when these "Sea People" came and overwhelmed the old civilization and left a new in its place. The Palestinian arts and crafts of that age are thus Cypriote. Egyptians also record the incoming of these "Sea Peoples" at this same time. The Israelites lost their arts and crafts in the sojourn in the wilderness. Thus, in the providence of God, these Palestinian

Upper: *TELL BEIT MIRSIM* FROM THE NORTH-EAST
Lower: THE "NETHER SPRING"

(Text on page 23)

PLATE I

Upper: **THE STAFF, 1926**
Left to right, Böhl, Albright, Kyle, Kelso, Webster, Lee, Dougherty
Lower: AN ARAB FAMILY BEFORE THEIR "SUMMER HOME"

(Text on page 37)

PLATE II

teachers were here to instruct the Israelites in the arts and crafts of a settled life. From this time onward for a long time, the Israelite pottery is of this Palestinian type.[1]

It is this very Palestinian pottery of Cypriote and Greek character, the pottery of the end of the Bronze Age and beginning of the Iron Age, which we must expect at Kirjath-sepher.[2] As the old prophet was told to take a potsherd and write upon it, so here in Palestine today, as in the Chinese articles at *Huis ten Bosch,* history is written upon the potsherds. To those who can read what is written, the old broken relics become fascinating.

PLANS AND PREPARATION

We had set March 14th for a visit to the site of our proposed excavations, but early in the morning, though it was not actually raining, and it did not threaten much rain, the clouds just came down and scraped along the ground and smeared up everything that can be smeared. It was like what the Californians call a "low fog"; the rain does not actually fall, because it is already down; it just settles on one and soaks clear through.

The next morning the sun rose bright and clear, and Neby Samwil lifted its head high into the bright sky. The clouds had gone up into the heavens, a sure sign of their lightness. The wiseacres said, "It will not rain today." The automobile came rushing up and we were off to find and explore Kirjath-sepher.

The great military road to Hebron and Beersheba winds and twists and turns among the Judean hills and we rushed along at about twenty-five miles an hour. In a few minutes we passed Rachel's tomb, so conspicuous in its loneliness, and Bethlehem and Beit Jala on their opposite hills making faces at each other. They are growing so rapidly that soon they will merge into one town and approach toward Jerusalem more rapidly, until before many years these towns will probably be no more than suburbs of the Holy City. Solomon's Pools and the new-old Hebron water supply—now as is the days of Pilate—furnish Jerusalem with water. This strangely links the dead past with the living present.

---

[1] For full discussion cf. ALBRIGHT, *Annual of American Schools of Oriental Research,* Vol. XII, pp. 53–56.
[2] ALBRIGHT, *Archaeology of Palestine and the Bible,* pp. 63 ff.

At last the automobile stopped before hotel Eshel Abraham in Hebron; we surrendered our bags to the porter and ourselves to the gentle guidance of a sturdy young Jewess, somewhat longer than she was broad, who showed us at once a "large upper room furnished." The floor stones were as cold as the stare Hebron Mohammedans give the "unbeliever," and the walls were that eternal duck-egg blue seen upon walls in this land. But the place was clean; not a flea! The food was abundant, if somewhat strange to a Christian's appetite. The water was excellent, and the talk almost anything wanted from bookish English to Hebrew, Arabic, and Yiddish. The cost of it all was two dollars and a half a day.

At the edge of town we had stopped a few minutes to pay our respects to Captain Bailey, the governor under the British mandate. The important posts under the mandate are filled by Englishmen—and filled well. We arranged to have a meeting with the land-owners at *Tell Beit Mirsim*, and then to meet their representative in the presence of the governor to sign a contract for lease of the land for excavations. We were glad to find again two of our old friends of the Sodom and Gomorrah explorations of 1924, Mr. Makhouli of the Palestine Antiquities Department, and Joseph, a helper in the American Mission at Kerak.

Leaving our luggage at the hotel and giving orders for dinner in the evening, we were soon off along the Beersheba road. The great buildings of the Russian hospice on the hill above Abraham's Oak, so-called, lift their mute witness to Heaven in protest against the iniquity of the Soviet government which has stopped nearly all the good work that the Russian church carried on. The hills in this part of Judea are stony and rugged, but the valleys are as rich as any in the world. What fields of wheat! No wonder the spies coming up from the desert were enthusiastic over this land.

In a little less than an hour we reached Dhahariyeh. We left our automobile here, took our raincoats, umbrellas, rubber shoes, and camera, not forgetting our lunch, and set off over the mountains and valleys and along muddy paths to *Tell Beit Mirsim*. Six miles there, and six miles back! It is important in all explorations in the world and in literature and philosophy to remember that we must come back. Some go so far that they fail to get back. Now nature intended to make me to be a walker, as everyone knows who has walked with me; I do not have to put my feet down as often as most people. And my natural strength did not abate on this journey. The way is indeed six miles as the crow flies; but nobody goes that way, and the way they go over the hills and down through the valleys, it is six very long Irish miles as I happen to know, for I walked it both ways that day. On the top of a high hill, with a glorious view of the Philistine Plain and the blue sea beyond, we rested and ate our lunch before reaching *Tell Beit Mirsim*.

On the hillside opposite the ruin we found the men of the neighborhood awaiting us. Among the mallows beside a wall they had spread rugs, as an honor to us, and there we sat while they crouched around; and the confabulation was on. They were a pleasant, genial lot. The conversation was rather general, interspersed with ringing laughter which told me matters were going on pleasantly. One of their number, the *mukhtar* of the group to which the owners belonged, undertook to negotiate with us, and it was arranged that the parties should meet before the governor in Hebron to make and sign the contract. With much hand-shaking and salaaming the interview was concluded, and we were at last free to cross the valley and examine the place we had come so far to see.

We were not disappointed. *Tell Beit Mirsim* is, indeed, a most promising ruin for examination. Here is an ideal fortified town, occupying a little oval-shaped conical hill entirely surrounded by deep valleys. Where a little neck of land joined this hill to the range on the south, a dry moat had been cut to complete the defences at that point. It is characteristically also a High Place, for on the north side the valley is about four hundred feet deep. There two broad valleys meet, one from the northeast and one from the northwest. The city occupied the whole top of the hill, approximately half a mile in circumference. The wall is still clearly visible nearly all the way around the precipitous sides of the hill. It is of heavy, somewhat regular, but undressed stone. A long, sloping revetment was outside and below the wall much of the way around. It was solidly made and with just the slope for defence from the wall above by bow and arrow.

We took a few pictures, and then "took up our carriages," which in this case consisted chiefly in lengthening our stride about six inches to shorten the return walk. We reached the automobile at Dhahariyeh, and just about sunset came in sight of the Vale of Mamre and then soon arrived at our hotel in Hebron. We had had a most successful day, and now a good dinner and a good sleep prepared us for the negotiations of the morrow. That dinner was a real one: an appetizer, a soup, sausage and fried potatoes, boiled pigeon which had already made the acquaintance of the soup before it now went to join it, a fruit relish, and wonderful jumbo Jaffa oranges. No wonder we slept.

Now began the sometimes nearly interminable bargaining and maneuvering of Oriental negotiations; the *mukhtar* was slow in coming, would not seem to hurry; then he was quite noncommittal, but finally agreed to meet us between two and three o'clock to go before the governor. Again he delayed. We waited until after three and then wrote a message deferring the negotiations to a later time to be arranged. *We would not seem to be in a hurry either!* To seem to hasten is only to prolong the bargaining. We go back to Jerusalem and in another week we may get through.

In fact the *mukhtar* soon announced that he was ready to sign the lease, and again we assembled at Hebron. Our first experience here now was the strange and not unpleasant one of running into the Passover customs of the Jews at the Hotel Eshel Abraham. These loyal Hebrews courageously extend their hospitality only in accord with the customs of the season. We had passover bread only. It looked like parchment, tasted like Scotch oatcake, and was not quite as slow of digestion as a pine shingle. While we ate, the family of the proprietor gathered about the table and chanted the ritual and drank the cups and were quite hilarious over it all. It is to them a joyous occasion.

Now another chapter of the seemingly endless delays of the Orient. The camels could be promised only for early Wednesday morning, and the governor was holding court on Tuesday and could not attend to us. There was nothing for us to do but to wait over Tuesday. We did some good exploring to satisfy ourselves about the actual site of the old city of Hebron. Indubitable evidence of the Early Bronze Age certified the fortress on the south hill "over against" the Cave of Machpelah. At last Wednesday came, but not the camels! We waited a while; then sent out to the market place to hire others. But they, alas, were out in pasture and must be fetched! At last, 10:30, the camels did come—and went away again! At 11:30 they came in full force and our goods were set out in parallel heaps between which the camels were made to kneel and were loaded. Dr. Albright got a horse which we promptly named Bucephalus. The rest of us with the *mukhtar* were to go by automobile. But now the automobile did not come. So we ate lunch, one more lunch in civilization before taking to the wilds. At 12:30 the camels did start and at 1 o'clock the automobile.

In the morning an astonishing bit of news had come: we were cordially invited to the enjoyment, the first night, of the hospitality of the *mukhtar* at his village near our place of work. Arab hospitality is not to be neglected, and especially must we begin well with the man who is our go-between, our daysman, if you please. We resigned ourselves, but I went out and ransacked the town until I found a box of Keating's powder!—good for whatever bites you.

Our journey down the Beersheba road was delightful, until we turned off it, and then we were at the end of our troubles—the beginning end! We went over some road intended only for a caterpillar tractor or an airplane. But a Palestine chauffeur and a Ford car can go over any road. At 5 p. m. we arrived at *Tell Beit Mirsim* and picked out a delightful place for camp, high and dry, with good air and with a fine view over the flower bedecked fields toward the "nether spring." At 6 o'clock we started on to the *mukhtar's* house along a charming valley through fields of lush wheat coming into head, until at last we came to the mountain side. There the car was abandoned; like Sisera, we went on our feet.

There was an evening of true patriarchal hospitality. The account of it is not entirely archæological, but it is part of the career of an archæologist, and it is important to know the whole story, else we may lose the perspective. The *mukhtar's* house was, in fact, a tent, a real Bedouin tent of black camel's hair cloth. It was about fifty feet long and twenty feet wide, with a dust floor and a fire of camel's dung burning in the center. About thirty men gathered to welcome us in a long reception line with the *mukhtar* in a white gown in the center. They brought two mattresses and two or three pillows for each of us and threw them down on the ground. I am sure these men robbed their own beds to give us comfort. Most of them lay down to sleep afterward on the bare ground with a stone for a pillow. All our goods were brought in and put beside us. When we were made comfortable, these men formed a long row and, with face to Mecca, said the fifth of the prayers of the day. They did not omit family prayers when they had guests. Then they asked what we would have to eat and drink, which was, of course, politeness, as they had already arranged our entertainment. They served us delicious Turkish coffee, then brought a big pot of excellent tea and hot milk and great round thin loaves of Arabic bread as large as the head of an apple barrel. I felt a little disappointed, as I had promised Dr. Wishart a feast. But I did my best; I drank quantities of tea, and ate a whole loaf of that Arabic bread, until I felt stuffed like a wheat bin. Then they served another coffee! I wrapped my traveling rug about me and dropped off to sleep.

Then Dr. Albright, who had tarried behind to see the tents set up and set a watch, came and informed us that what we had eaten was only an appetizer and that the feast was still to come! Shades of gormands, how were we to eat any more? Yet, if we were to be archæologists in this community, we must accept the hospitality of the people and do justice to it. The feast came about 10:15. Heaped dishes of rice, and a great platter of rice with a boiled kid on top, a dish of chopped meat brazed, a dip seasoned with some sort of Arab limburger, bowls of stewed vegetables, and a pudding for dessert, and tea, more tea. We ate! Then we had another cup of coffee, this time bitter Arabic coffee. And, at least, the welcome announcement. "Now, gentlemen, you may sleep." That "may" was better grammar than we knew at that moment. After all that tea and coffee, I hardly slept a wink until 3 o'clock. There was not a flea, "nor nothing," and my hunt for Keating's powder had been

futile on this occasion. Dr. Wishart remarked that he would
not have missed that night's experience for anything. It is
indeed worth much archæologically to have such a patriarchal experience.

We started to camp next morning about 7 o'clock. It was
the time of the fast of Ramadan, when there is nothing to
eat or drink in a Mohammedan household until after sunset;
so we went off without breakfast. This lack we endeavored
to supply by the fragments of a lunch which we had provided for the day before. But what cared we; we were
actually at last going to begin to dig, to find things! And
before we arrived, almost before we had well started the
finding began; we came to the "upper spring," a great valley
well fifty feet down to the water and twelve feet across and
with indubitable marks of age that put it long before Caleb's
time. We soon reached camp and about nine o'clock began
to dig.

How the Archæologist Knows

To many people, the work of the archæologist seems
much like the doings of a fortune teller or a necromancer.
It may be well to make clear that the archæologist does not
belong at all among such uncanny folk. The work of the
archæologist is not a guess. Some think it nothing more than
just that. They look on the work of the archæologist as so
many do on the skill of the physician; they think the whole
medical claim to knowledge is mere guesswork. So they
go around from one physician to another; *one guess is as
good as another.* Exactly so, not a few people think that
the archæologist guesses where to dig, then guesses what he
has found and what it means. They do not discriminate
among reports and opinions either; for "is not one guess as
good as another"?

Now all this is wrong. Except for a few mountebanks,
who creep into every profession, neither physicians nor
archæologists guess at anything. The physician is guided
by *symptoms* and *experiment,* and the archæologist is
guided in exactly the same way. Ruins always have "symptoms." A *"tell"* is an artificial heap made up of the ruins of
a city and a civilization. The archæologist does not dig out
in the open field, but where the "symptoms" are. A wall, a

chimney, fragments of pottery scattered over the surface of the ground, these and a hundred other things that man has made, indicate where to dig. Then, having found the "symptoms," the archæologist also experiments. He stirs the surface a little to see what civilization is represented there. This tells him when the place was finally abandoned, for the last ruins will be on top. Then, perhaps he digs a test trench down through the ruins to the bottom. At the bottom, he will find the beginnings of civilization which have left anything at that place. Between the top and the bottom will appear all the layers of civilizations which destructions have left.

In all Bible lands, these various civilizations lie in layers exactly like the strata in a stone quarry. All the western world clears away the rubbish to virgin soil or to bedrock before building. In Bible lands it was not so. Each civilization built immediately on top of that which had been destroyed. It is this that makes the science of archæology possible and really historical.

Thus the work of the archæologist is not a mere "gamble." He does not know in any detail what he will find, and in that sense "it is the unexpected that happens" in his career. But his work is as reliable and confident as that of the scientific miner. The miner finds the vein, tests its character and follows its drift. He only does *not* know how the vein will hold out in quality. So the archæologist locates the ruin, determines its character, and follows the various "veins" that lie there. Only he does *not* know the quality of the product which the ruin will yield nor whether or not a vein will "hold out" all the way through, or the strata prove to have been disturbed.

At the east wall of ancient Heliopolis, in 1912, Professor Petrie found the gateway and located the foundation deposit all carefully arranged and filled with clean sand in due order, but when he put his hand in the sand for the relics deposited there, the place had been robbed! In 1924, at the ruin of Zoar of Arabian times, at the lower end of the Dead Sea, we dug down to the bottom of the ruins to find, if we might, the remains of the town in the days of Lot. Alas, the ruins reached virgin soil at Byzantine times! not a trace of any earlier civilization. It was disappointing at the time, but when we finally found the remains of the ancient civilization of the time of Abraham and Lot, we realized the meaning of the silence of the Bible history about this region after the destruction of the doomed cities. The region was so utterly destroyed that for twenty-five hundred years there was no civilization of any kind on the Plain; not indeed until climatic influences had washed out the salt and sulphur. So, though it was "the unexpected that happened" in our researches there, after all there was no gambling in our work, but only scientific discovery.

In fact, the work of the archæologist is thoroughly scientific work. In the work planned for Kirjath-sepher, there will first be made the most careful search and examination of various sites to ascertain, if possible, which one is truly the site of this ancient city. There are many *tells*, ruined cities, in south Palestine. Most of them were destroyed by Nebuchadnezzar, when that ruthless monarch swept like a besom of destruction over this region, after, in fury, he had destroyed Jerusalem and the Temple and then had set out to reduce the whole land to helplessness by systematic frightfulness. Most of these towns in the southern part of the land then destroyed have never been rebuilt.

The method of excavation will also be systematic and scientific. A short time ago a gentleman said to me, "If you had a steam shovel that I saw at work a few days ago, you could soon excavate that town." That method would do, if we only wanted to make a hole in the ground or dig a long ditch. But since we wish to *find* things, even the least trifle, such scoop shovel methods would be fatal. The layers of civilization in the *tell* would all be mixed together from the bottom to the top and dumped in a heap. Imagine!

Instead of such a method, men are employed with little hoes to turn over every bit of debris carefully and often to put it into a sieve to be sifted. Then boys with baskets carry away the rubbish. Each layer of history is taken off carefully; everything found is examined carefully; the place of its finding carefully noted and charted; all buildings and walls put into a carefully surveyed plan; all articles photographed and catalogued, so that exact comparisons may be made. When the whole of a layer of ruins has been removed from the portion under examination, the next layer below is then attacked and treated in the same way. Thus the work goes on till the whole ruin has been examined.

Movable things all belong to the Department of Antiquities. But the government, in order to stimuate private investment in this work for which Palestine has yet but small funds, promises a division of the movable finds, giving about one half to those who do the work. It is usual to allot the share thus allowed the excavators among those contributing considerable sums to the work, or to give them the right to designate where the relics shall go.

Now about this place, Kirjath-sepher, we do know a great many things. We know that it was a place of considerable importance in the Conquest days, and was assigned to the family of Caleb, one of the great leaders under Joshua. We do know that it has had three names of old, Kirjath-sannah (Instruction-town), Debir[3] (Oracle), and Kirjath-sepher (Writing-town or Book-town). We do know that archæologists have long thus had the opinion that there was here a school, a temple with an oracle, and a library. We do know also that all this region and probably this city was destroyed by Nebuchadnezzar and not rebuilt, and so all the relics sealed up from that time onward, and thus safe from further destruction from man. We do know that the Israelites, at the time this city was assigned to the family of Caleb, had but recently come out of the wilderness wanderings, having left Moses, their great leader, at Nebo. We do know that Moses wrote; how much is a matter of dispute, but the Pentateuch claims him as author of most of it and tradition from ancient times ascribes all the remainder to him.

Finally we do know that the literary method of writing for all Palestinian documents at that time was the cuneiform script, and in the Babylonian tongue written by native scribes, and upon clay tablets. We do not know that we shall find any such tablets at Kirjath-sepher, but we do know the expectation of archæologists that clay tablets were once there; they are not very perishable and we hope to find some of them there yet. In any case, we will learn much concerning the events and the products of that city in Conquest times, and so get much light upon Israelite history of

3) *Joshua* 15:49; 15:15;*Judges* 1:11.

the entrance into the Promised Land and, in general, gain a knowledge of that culture of Bible lands which is indeed the matrix of Bible narratives.

Now we must see the evidence that this place at *Tell Beit Mirsim* really is Kirjath-sepher. Though the complete identification came out little by little in the course of the work, it is better for the reader that it be placed here all together at the outset. Dhahariyeh, a small town on the Hebron-Beersheba road, has long been identified as Kirjath-sepher, and is so marked on all the maps,[4] and so described by Dr. George Adam Smith in his *Historical Geography of the Holy Land*. A very cursory examination of this place in the light of present-day knowledge of Palestinian archæology serves to show that there is not a single item of evidence to sustain this identification, unless it be its convenience of access for explorers and tourists! There is absolutely no *tell*, no heap of ruins, which an ancient walled city always leaves. The location is not at all suitable, or even reasonably possible, for a walled city; it is not on an isolated hill, but on a long ridge impossible of fortification in the ancient fashion, and there is not the slightest indication that any attempt has ever been made so to fortify it. Great walls ten feet thick and forty feet high do not run away; they stay put. They are not here, therefore they never were here. There is no good water source; the place is, indeed, notorious for its bad water. The "so-called upper and nether springs" pointed out by Dr. Smith as fulfilling the topographical requirements of Kirjath-sepher, are not adequate true sources at all, but mainly artificial sources, cisterns and reservoirs for rainwater, as are all those at Dhahariyeh. Dr. Albright in his tireless topographical researches in Palestine, when he set out to search the "south country" in the territory of Judah for some other site that supplied at least some of the qualifications for identification as Kirjath-sepher, selected the site at *Tell Beit Mirsim;* the progress of the work has now completed the evidence for the identification as follows:

A. ARCHÆOLOGICAL IDENTIFICATION

I. The Israelites came into Palestine near the beginning of the Early Iron Age and continued in the land to the end

---

[4] SMITH, *Atlas of Historical Geography*, Map 12.

of it. At the time of the Conquest, the name of the last walled city of south Judah taken by the Israelites was Debir; but "The name of Debir before was Kirjath-sepher."[5] This does not necessarily mean that the Israelites changed the name of the place, nor that it was named Debir exactly at that period, but only that it was so called at the time the account in Joshua and Judges was written, and that the name formerly had been Kirjath-sepher, but how long "before" there is no indication. We are only told that before the Conquest the place was called Kirjath-sepher. This would be in Canaanite times. Thus, wherever Kirjath-sepher may be located, it must show Canaanite history of one or more of the Bronze Ages. This requirement is satisfied, and more than satisfied, at *Tell Beit Mirsim*. Here are the remains of not only the Late and the Middle Bronze Ages, but of the Early Bronze Age also back at least beyond 2000 B. C. Père Vincent believes it to go back much nearer the middle of the third millennium B. C. Thus there is here at this place a Canaanite history of at least 700 years and probably much more.

II. Any site that is to be identified as Kirjath-sepher must have been assailed and destroyed sufficiently to be taken about the beginning of the Early Iron Age, as that was the time of the Israelite Conquest and Debir was taken by Othniel.[6] And except for this account in the Bible we do not know anything definite about the location of Kirjath-sepher. Now destruction at that time is clearly shown here. A gruesome burned layer occurs in the stratification at this level. Everything below this layer of ashes is Canaanite and everything above is Israelite.

III. Then the site that is to be identified with Kirjath-sepher must have been occupied by Israelites during the whole of the national period from the Conquest to the Exile, i. e., from the beginning of the Early Iron Age I to the end of Early Iron II; for the Israelites are represented to have occupied Debir at the Conquest and this part of the land did not cease to be Jewish until the destruction and deportation wrought by Nebuchadnezzar about 600 B. C. Now this place at *Tell Beit Mirsim* was so occupied during this whole

[5] *Joshua* 15:15; *Judges* 1:11.
[6] *Joshua* 15:13–19; *Judges* 1:12–15.

period as the pottery shows. Indeed, it was rebuilt some time very soon after the Conquest. *At least the site was occupied.*

IV. Then the place identified as Kirjath-sepher must have been destroyed near the end of Early Iron Age II, as were "the fenced cities of Judah" by Nebuchadnezzar. This place was destroyed at that time and was never again rebuilt.

V. Like other fenced cities in this part of the land, Kirjath-sepher should show no rebuilding in the post-exilic period. And we find that here at *Tell Beit Mirsim* the whole course of civilization has rested at 600 B. C. There is no trace of any later occupation until Byzantine times, 600 A. D. (and but very little then)—a period of 1200 years. Here is to be found no trace of Greek, Maccabean, or Roman occupation.

Thus every archæological requirement for Kirjath-sepher is fulfilled here at *Tell Beit Mirsim.*

B. Topographical Identification

I. Kirjath-sepher must be found in a district of the Shephelah between the sea-plain and Hebron in which only three important fenced cities were located, Lachish, Eglon and Kirjath-sepher. The account in Joshua calls for only these. This place at *Tell Beit Mirsim* lies in that region.

II. Kirjath-sepher must have been either well to the right, or well to the left, of a direct way from Lachish, to Hebron, for the line of march was from Lachish *back to Hebron* before going to Kirjath-sepher. But Lachish is placed by Eusebius six miles south of *Beit Jibrin.* There is no site *well to the north of this line of march; Tell Beit Mirsim* is *well to the south.*

III. Of the two important ruins well to the south of the line of march from Lachish to Hebron, *Tell Beit Mirsim* and *Tell el-Khuweilifeh, Tell Beit Mirsim* only is in the territory of Judah, to which Debir belonged. *Tell el-Khuweilifeh* is certainly in the territory of Simeon, and besides fails to qualify in nearly every other respect.[7]

---

[7] Albright, *Archæology of Palestine and the Bible*, p. 79.

IV. Kirjath-sepher was located near the edge of the Negeb, the south country. It was a "south land." So is this.

V. Kirjath-sepher was in the land of the Anakim, the giants, as were also Hebron and Anab, a city five miles southeast of *Tell Beit Mirsim*. That is, they were in the land of Cyclopean or Titanic building. Here is much of the great stone work of the early Canaanites at *Tell Beit Mirsim*.

VI. Finally, Kirjath-sepher, or Debir, has the specific topographical marking given in Joshua and Judges.[8]—"And Caleb said, He that smiteth Kirjath-sepher, and taketh it, to him will I give Achsah my daughter to wife. And Othniel the son of Kenaz, Caleb's younger brother, took it; and he gave him Achsah his daughter to wife. And it came to pass, when she came to him, that she moved him to ask of her father a field, and she lighted from off her ass; and Caleb said unto her, What wilt thou? And she said unto him, Give me a blessing: for thou hast given me a south land; give me also springs of water. And Caleb gave her the upper springs and the nether springs." It had "upper springs, and nether springs," two sources of water supply which could be so described. The word used here in the Hebrew text is not *ain,* the ordinary word for spring, but a word used very seldom in the Hebrew Bible, *gullah* (plural *gulloth*) meaning "receptacle." It is not the word for a surface spring at all, but for some kind of well.

Now *Tell Beit Mirsim* has just such *gulloth,* "upper and nether springs." The upper great one is a large valley well about a mile and a half north of the *tell* and toward the mountains, the "upper" country. The other great one is about one mile south of the *tell* down toward the Negeb. The people of the neighborhood still describe these directions as "upper" and "lower," and naturally so. These wells were surrounded by other less important ones. These two, at least, are very old. The running of the ropes in the drawing of water in the course of centuries wears deep grooves in the hard limestone of the well curb. In time also the accumulation of dust around the well becomes so deep that a new well curb is needed. After centuries more these new curbstones will be grooved also. *Six successive well curbs are at the top of each of these wells,* each in turn worn into

---

8) *Joshua* 15:13–19; *Judges* 1:12–15. Cf. *Joshua* 10:34–30

deep grooves sometimes three or four inches deep. The topmost curb-stones of the "nether" spring were thrown down by the British during the war, when they put a pump into the well, but the stones still lie beside the well. The age of these wells as indicated by these successive well curbs can only be estimated in millenniums. If these wells were not here and were somewhere else, we would then see what a black shadow even a well may cast. The "nether spring" being nearest us, furnished us with excellent water during our work.

Thus every archæological requirement, and every topographical requirement, for the identification of Kirjath-sepher is completely met here. No other suggested site satisfactorily supplies any of them, not even Dhahariyeh, which has received so much recognition as to be placed upon the maps as Debir. However, it is one thing to have a good case and be sure of the evidence, but sometimes quite another thing to convince all the jury. It is still suggested in some quarters that, after all, Dhahariyeh is the real site of Kirjath-sepher. In order to satisfy all the jury, careful soundings were later made at Dhahariyeh. Thirteen pits carefully distributed around the border and through the town were sunk to the mountain top and the results carefully noted and compared. Nearly all these pits came to the rock at one and a half to two and a half meters of depth; in only one was the depth four meters. Nowhere was any trace of city walls found, except Roman walls and these not walls of circumvallation. Nor indeed were great house walls found nor many walls of any character. A very little pottery of the Early Iron Age II was found showing some occupation of the site in the times of the Kings of Judah. Hardly any pottery of Early Iron I was found; of Late Bronze and Middle Bronze nothing whatever. It was thus not occupied at all for many centuries before the Israelites came in. In the Early Bronze Age there was evidence of a camping place, perhaps a village, but no trace of a wall.

Thus results of this careful examination fully corroborate our former conclusion from archæological and topographical data that neither Kirjath-sepher nor any other walled city was ever built at this place. There was no fortification of any kind until Roman times, and then in a way entirely different from the fenced cities of the Canaanites.

Visitors viewing the excavations are wont to say, "Well, there is a lot of imagination about it," by which they mean that, to their mind, it is mostly imagination. Now there is "a lot of imagination" in the interpretation given by archæologists, but it is the imagination that sees things as they were and not that sees things that never were. There is the historical imagination by which one places himself in the environment of historical personages and sees things round about them as they saw them. Then there is the mathematical imagination of the surveyor. He finds a fragment of wall and takes its bearing to a second. Presently another fragment of wall appears a little farther on which has exactly the same bearing. The surveyor projects the line of that wall from one fragment to the other. Another wall is found exactly parallel and then a fragment of a crosswall at right angles. The projection of these lines gives the outline of a room, a house, and then one house after another, in like manner, until the whole plan of that part of the city has appeared. Here the imagination is a mathematical imagination. Thus the historian and the surveyor construct history and the work of the archæologist becomes a real historical science, as exact as any other historical science.

But another element enters into this work. At one place is a piece of wall or a corner. The top of that fragment seems to belong to the wall we are tracing, but when the surveyor sets the level, at the bottom of that fragment, it is revealed as belonging to a totally different stratum and in alignment with other walls of that different stratum of the ruins. It is of a different age, and must be projected on a plan of an entirely different level. Thus each stratum of the *tell*, representing as it does a different city, is surveyed and leveled and planned. So the work of the surveyor turns what seems to some, vague imagination, into exact mathematical science.

ORGANIZATION OF THE STAFF

The organization of the staff is each season a task of great responsibility; for upon this depends much of the success of the work, and especially the satisfaction which it gives to the world of scholars, and the impression made by the expedition upon Bible students everywhere. Failure to take account of this may mean disaster, however much is really done. It is especially gratifying, therefore, to introduce in the appropriate place the staff for each campaign at *Tell Beit Mirsim*.

It is the ambition and aim to assemble a staff of distinguished specialists for each season. In fact the modern conception of a first class archæological expedition is not merely an enthusiastic company of curiosity seekers on a scientific junket—it always has something of that exuberant character—but also a school of training that, while its task is to discover and discuss, is also to cultivate specialists in Bible lands lore, all of which rests upon the idea, so trite among field archæologists here and so little known in the homeland, that *no true Orientalist can be made in the Occident. The* atmosphere there is fatal; the Bible is an Oriental book which can be seen aright only by eyes that have acquired the Oriental focus and stigmatism. We have only to observe the Oriental in America or Europe to understand from his blunders how little the Occidental with his western conception of things fits into the Oriental life.

In addition to this fundamental difference between the Orient and the Occident, this Land of the Book is a land of startling paradoxes; with about 150 kinds of trees, it is still a treeless land; with some 300 kinds of birds, it is often said to be a land without birds. There are here some of the most beautiful buildings, public and private, in the world and elegant houses being constantly erected, yet round about our work in *Tell Beit Mirsim* the country people live during the whole season of their crops in caves and holes in the ground; they are still troglodytes. The village of *Beit Mirsim* on the hill east of us is almost wholly of this character.

The campaign of 1926 was undertaken by Xenia Theological Seminary in coöperation with the American School of Oriental Research at Jerusalem. As President of Xenia Seminary, I was President of the Staff. The Director of field operations was Dr. William F. Albright, Director of the American School of Oriental Research. The other members of the Staff were Prof. James L. Kelso, of Xenia Seminary,

Prof. John E. Wishart of San Francisco Seminary, Prof. F. M. Th. Böhl of Groningen University, Holland, and two students of the Graduate School of Xenia Seminary, Rev. A. W. Webster and Rev. James R. Lee.

With our competent camp staff of cook and waiter and watchman and soldier-guard we pitched our tents amidst the flower-bedecked grain fields and settled ourselves to our task.

CHAPTER II

BEGINNINGS

Camp *Tell Beit Mirsim.*

THE history of ceramics in Palestine, and with it also the value of ceramics in the history of Palestinian civilization, has been well worked out. The foundation of this science for Palestine was laid by Professor, now Sir William Flinders Petrie at *Tell el-Hesy.* There, by a complete exposure of the strata, he was able satisfactorily to determine the types of pottery which belong to each Age of Palestinian history. Since the work at *Tell el-Hesy,* many other tests have been made until now the types which characterize the various ages are well known, and the science of pottery chronology has become about as exact as any historical science can be. As a piece of Delft ware or a fragment of the delicate china of Limoges immediately indicates the period of European history of civilization to which it belongs, so the various types of Palestinian pottery indicate as certainly and as clearly the age of Palestinian history of civilization from which they come. The Ages have been classified as follows with some slight variation in dates by different archæologists:

The Early Bronze Age, 3000 to 2000 B. C.
The Middle Bronze Age, 2000 to 1600 B. C.
The Late Bronze Age, 1600 to 1200 B. C.
The Early Iron Age I, 1200 to 900 B. C.
The Early Iron Age II, 900 to 600 B. C.
The Early Iron Age III, 600 to 300 B. C.

The finding of these different types characterizes the different strata, but does not date them. The determining of the dates of these various ages has required an additional item of evidence. In these different strata in which the types prevail there are found also Egyptian and Babylonian remains which can be dated. Thus the stratum in which the find is made is also given a date. Finally the evidence is completed by the invariable habit in ancient Palestine of rebuilding directly upon the top of the rubbish of ruins instead of clearing the ground as in the western world.

A kind of necessary preliminary now to any successful work of excavation in Palestine at any given site, is thus to determine the stratification. Accordingly very early in our work at Kirjath-sepher — for we may now confidently call this place by that name — we chose a level place inside the city walls and made a cutting right down to virgin soil as a first study. Later this was fortified by a second and much larger cutting and the results carefully measured and recorded.

It is, of course, a necessary characteristic of all examination of stratification that it must begin at the top and go down to the bottom, must thus begin at the latest point in the history of the site and follow the stream of history back to its source. Thus the end of the history at Kirjath-sepher in its destruction by Nebuchadnezzar naturally does not appear distinctly in this stratification; especially since the elements have long ago destroyed over the surface the evidence of the burning which took place at that time; only at other points, as in the chambers of the gateway, has that been found. The remainder of the debris which forms the present stratification may be described as follows:

Though the examination necessarily took place from the top to the bottom, the description will be best understood, if made from the bottom to the top, from the earliest period onward. At the bottom of the stratification was a thin layer, about half a meter, of debris containing Early Bronze Age, and early Middle Bronze Age pottery, the ledge-handle and the rope ornament of the heavy Early Bronze Age pottery, and the thinner, and much more beautiful, reddish yellow pottery of the Middle Bronze Age. At the end of this comparatively brief period of the history, and close to 1800 B. C., is a layer of burned material; destruction of the city has been attempted by fire. There is, as yet, no historical written record of any such destruction at Kirjath-sepher, or at any other place in Palestine. But it is most significant that wherever in the excavations at different sites this age has been reached, this stratum of burning appears. It is most suggestive also, and tempting to a spirit of speculation, to note that this is also the period of the Hyksos invasion of Egypt. Whether or not there is any connection between these historical events it is impossible to say, but it is equally significant that the historical record of the Patriarchs of that period makes them turn to these same Hyksos, when in distress in the land of Palestine.. The Hyksos were friendly to them.

Above this layer of ashes are three other such layers separated from each other by layers of debris as follows: the first about two meters deep, the second a thin layer of about one-fourth meter, the third about two meters. The distance from this last burning to the surface is about two and a half meters. This last denotes probably a longer period of rest for the city than either of the other strata. It is not possible to say with absolute positiveness who burned the city at these various times, except it be the second. But the comparative depth of the various layers of debris and the historical knowledge which we have from Egyptian inscriptions as well as from Biblical records make the following account attain almost to historical certainty.

The account in the Bible of the invasion of Palestine by the Egyptians in the days of the beginning of the divided monarchy reveals Shishak, a Libyan, on the throne of Egypt, who pillaged the fenced cities of Judah.[1] Shishak himself leaves a record of this same pillage of Palestinian cities in an inscription on the south wall of one of the temples at Karnak.[2] Unfortunately a part of his list of names is utterly destroyed. Kirjath-sepher does not appear in the portion of the list yet remaining. Whether or not it was among those names destroyed it is impossible to say, but here is a stratum of burning back a long time before the final destruction by Nebuchadnezzar about 600 B. C. and the pottery found immediately above this burning and immediately below it puts this burning undoubtedly at that period, about the time of Rehoboam and Jeroboam. Two other burnings are, as I have said, closer together and cover about two meters of debris altogether. They represent shorter periods of time. When the Israelites came into the land a very great battle was necessary for the taking of Kirjath-sepher by "the whole army." [3] The immediate commander was Othniel.[4] The Late Bronze Age and the

---

[1] *II Chron.* 12:4.
[2] SMITH's *Bible Dictionary*, IV, p. 3013 f, with transliteration. MULLER, *Egyptological Researches*, 1906.
[3] *Joshua* 10:28–39.
[4] *Joshua* 15:13–19.

Early Iron Age merge into each other; Canaanite history crosses the line and so does Israelite history. Yet *here* everything below this line of ashes is Canaanite and everything above it is Israelite. As there was a change of culture, there must have been a conquest; as the change of culture was from Canaanite to Israelite, the conquest must have been by Israelites; and as there was immediate occupation which continued by Israelites to the end of the national life, this conquest must have been that of the time of Joshua. So that this great catastrophe to the city may confidently be set down to Othniel and the incoming of the Israelites.

Now the identification of the destroyer responsible for the still remaining layer of ashes, between that of Othniel and that of Shishak, has still less to determine it. The only hint we have is that Cushan-rishathaim oppressed Israel while Othniel was still living and he, during his judgeship,[5] led Israel in driving away the oppressor and delivering from his oppression. As this burning occurs after a thin layer of debris from the last preceding one at the incoming of Israel, it is possible that Cushan-rishathaim came to Othniel's city and besieged it and at least partly destroyed it, but was finally defeated and driven off by Othniel.

Thus the stratification of Kirjath-sepher gives the most complete conspectus of Palestinian history to be found at any one site thus far excavated, extending as it does from about 2000 B. C. (a little before the time of Abraham) down to 600 B. C. and the destruction by Nebuchadnezzar. It covers about 700 years of Canaanite history and consecutively the whole period of Israelite history, approximately 700 years, from the Conquest of Canaan to the Babylonian Exile.

TRACING THE WALLS

The spies sent out by Moses probably came right by this city-crowned summit, since Kirjath-sepher lies near the head of one of the broadest and most beautiful of the valleys that run up from the south country, the Negeb, into the Shephelah, the hill country, and the mountains of Judea. What did they see? They reported "cities . . . . walled up to heaven." Was this one of them? Our ideas of ancient civi-

---

[5] *Judges* 3:8–11.

lization from reading the Biblical allusions alone are often very meagre, for the Bible rarely ever describes things minutely, but only sufficiently for the purpose of the Book, and we are apt to be surprised when the work of the archæologists confronts us with all the facts. It is so at Kirjath-sepher. The brief allusions to a city with a "field" and with "upper" and "nether springs" captured by Othniel, Caleb's young nephew, raises little or no expectation. Our work thus far, though only begun, has already filled in the details of the picture until a great fortress crowning an almost impregnable hilltop has appeared surrounded on every side by valleys deep and fertile.

The wall was plainly to be seen almost all the way around the circumference of the city before we began work. We naturally took what appeared to be the top of the wall as really that and expected to trace the wall thence down to the foundations. Our first surprise was to discover that it was the bottom of the *wall still left standing* which we saw at nearly every point of the circle of the city, merely the foundation stones at the *ground level within the walls*. The outcome of the sieges of these ancient cities was apt to be like the description of the termination of the siege of Jericho: "The wall fell down flat." [6] It was indeed a ruthless warfare which so destroyed that which must immediately be rebuilt before being appropriated to the use of the conquerors. We quickly traced nearly the whole circle of the wall on the outside and, in part, on the inside. How high it was we have as yet no indication from the ruins, and judging from the experience at other excavations, we are not likely to get any.

The ruthlessness and fierceness of the destruction wrought by old conquerors is only beginning to be fully understood as we try to reconstruct that which they pulled down. The strength of the defences may be understood from the the fact that it took four men and two boys, with all the tools necessary and no enemy opposing, two hours to get out the first stone from the great revetment wall, and a full half day to breach that wall by a hole some three or four feet square. Behind this revetment was a filling of beaten earth fifteen feet deep at the bottom and sloping up to the parapet; then back

---

[6] *Joshua* 6:20.

of all this was the *great Canaanite wall* quite substantially built of stone, at least ten feet thick on the average.

The wall was very skillfully constructed! indeed, we are discovering day by day, with admiration, the evidence of this skill. It would seem as though every engineering device known to military science today was used by those who planned and built this wall. It is an almost continuous series of towers and buttresses, and what in modern fortifications would be called embrasures, so arranged as to give an enfilading fire. The opportunity thus afforded was doubtless as useful for arrows and slingstones as now for cannon and machine guns and rifles.

Nearly the whole circuit of the wall was strengthened by the revetment, much of which is still preserved *in situ* and fit for use. These exterior defenses were largely constructed of sections of convex curves, so as to give again an opportunity for enfilading, as well as to strengthen the stonework. The stones were pointed inward and downward toward the focus of an ellipse thus taking advantage of the principle of the arch. Usually these outer defenses reached down to a supporting terrace of the hill, sometimes two rods distant, but on the north side of the hill the declivity was so steep that no such terrace was within reach. Here the wall was strong at the top and protected with a continuous revetment supported at the bottom by a retaining wall. At first this looked like two walls, but soon the true character appeared. At one point steps led up and over this revetment, and a strong buttress or tower was placed at the head of the stairs for protection.

Great numbers of slingstones and weavers' weights, used at times in the same manner as slingstones, are found around the outside of the wall. These slingstone finds doubtless represent all sieges from that of Othniel, and even long before, down to the final destruction by the devastating host of Nebuchadnezzar.

From the brief historical and descriptive account of Debir in the Bible it would seem to have been chiefly an Israelite city, with only a hint of a pre-Israelite career, when it was known as Kirjath-sepher. Since the pottery everywhere about the ruins ends with the stratum of Israelite remains of about 600 B. C., it seems practically certain that this city was finally destroyed at the time the host of Nebuchadnezzar swept over

Upper: SECTION OF THE "A" LEVEL, SHOWING HOUSE WALLS, CASE-MATES AND CITY WALL

Lower: A CUTTING MADE IN THE REVET-MENT TO SHOW ITS CONSTRUCTION

(Text on page 48)

PLATE III

southern Palestine. While some Byzantine sherds are found on the surface, there is nothing between these and those, and no Byzantine buildings at all have been discovered.

When we began to dig around about the wall and the gateway it soon appeared that these present remains so plainly visible were all Israelitish and so the ruins represented Israelite history from the earliest Israelite occupation down to 600 B. C. But as soon as we dug toward the foundation of the walls and the gateway, and through a layer of ashes and other evidences of burning, we came upon pottery of the Late Bronze Age, 1600 to 1200 B. C., then upon pottery of the Middle Bronze Age, 2000 to 1600 B. C., and below this stratum, pottery of the Early Bronze Age of 2000 B. C. or earlier. In any case the name Kirjath-sepher certainly stands for a long Canaanite history; how long we may never know. Certainly this site may rank as one of the earliest cities in Palestine and it is seen that the brief allusion to the city as "before" called Kirjath-sepher covers a very much longer period than was supposed.

Now it will be seen that the record of the stages of history of this old city are opened at the great gateway like the pages of a book. Naturally we had to begin our investigations at the surface representing the latest history and go down to the virgin soil where people began to build. At the bottom here some six feet of debris were filled with Bronze Age pottery, some Early Bronze, a good deal of Middle Bronze, and Late Bronze, and down to the beginning of the Iron Age, the Israelite period of history in this land. This lower part of the ruins here represents the Patriarchal Age from the time of Abraham, and perhaps before, down to the incoming of the Israelites under Joshua.

On top of this stratum was a gruesome stratum of burned material — ashes, charcoal, lime, and burned stone. These old Canaanites built in stone — and great stone; it was the time of the Anakim, the giants, and they were Titanic builders. This stratum of burned material is rather difficult to measure exactly, but in the compressed state in which it is now to be seen it is about six inches. It runs right through from one side near the great gateway to the other. What tragic scenes have been, not embalmed, but incinerated here! How vivid a commentary have these ashes written upon the attack by Othniel, the young nephew of Caleb! He was fighting to win a wife, as well as to take a city. When we see the devastation wrought, we understand the strength and importance of this old fortress which induced Caleb to offer so great a reward to the leader in Israel who could take it.

Above this burned layer began, of course, the Israelite period, the Iron Age. For from this level up to the top every bit of pottery was Israelite and the weapons and implements iron. As the final conflagration had caused everything from the top to fall down into the rooms and passageways at the gate, the different stages of Israelite history were mixed together in the ruins at that point, but they were all there, from the earliest times, when the Israelites were in contact with the Philistines and learned from them, down to the characteristic pots with ribbed handles, so common in the period of the kings. From the debris round about the gate these different ages could be clearly distinguished.

The Gates

What may have been the exact character of the Canaanite defenses at the gate is impossible now to say. Whether, indeed, Othniel destroyed entirely the stone work, which would mean that it was afterward entirely rebuilt by the Israelites, or whether much of the stonework of the gate was left when all the woodwork was burned, meaning that the stone walls still standing represent in large part the old Canaanite work, it is impossible accurately to determine. Probably in some part the older work was re-used. The defenses as the Israelites rebuilt them are plainly visible. There was a great fortress on the east of the gate with a tower topped with mud brick. Curiously these mud bricks are astonishingly like Ramesside bricks of Egypt. West of this tower was a small room apparently with no entrance from without. Then in the center was the entrance to the city with a square turning to make it easy of defense. West of this was another room and another tower smaller than on the east, or it may have been only a strong bastion. This part of the gateway also was topped with mud brick. This great Israelite gate was completely burned about 600 B. C., probably by Nebuchadnezzar. Great heaps of ashes, charcoal, lime from calcined stone, and even half-burned stone were found on the pavement of the entrance and of the rooms. The towers were about three meters wide on the front, and the walls in the gateway, like the city wall, of this period were about four feet thick.

We make many discoveries, but sometimes the finds are rather surprising, sometimes disappointing episodes. Here is one such. We learned at the very outset that this place was not rebuilt after the time of Nebuchadnezzar. It does not prove to be exact to conclude, however, that there were never any building operations on the hill, even though the city was not rebuilt. For three days a curious serpentine wall came out near the west gate. A plain open place was in front of it toward the gate. We had visions of a somewhat ornate plaza with perhaps public buildings in the center. Alas when the "plaza" was excavated a whole system of walls appeared underneath covering the space, and the serpentine wall ran over the top of them with utter disregard of rooms or corners. Evidently the serpentine wall was built after the city was in ruins; it was not a rebuilding of the city, but only a farm-wall put up by the post-exilic folk to enclose a little field for cultivation! The serpentine form follows the ancient method of Canaanite wall building; it was stronger than a straight wall. The method is still used by our workmen, probably not knowing why. How seldom do people know the why of community customs. It is interesting to come thus unexpectedly upon the work of the people of the days of Ezra and Nehemiah.

Of course, a walled city must have gates; and a great city, great gates. They made one on the east and one on the west at Kirjath-sepher. The one on the east was the stopping-place of a great roadway which still stretches for miles across the mountains and everywhere is marked by the big stones of Canaanite masonry, and indeed, is still used in many places, — used now by the explorers in going back and forth. The west gate opened out at a point where the valleys sloped away, both to the north and to the south, and thus that gate opened to the north, the west, and the south.

How great was the building at that early east gateway one may only surmise from the greatness of its foundation, for nothing else of it is now visible. It has either been utterly destroyed or has completely disappeared in subsequent building. But we do know that disaster overtook this first gateway and the first great wall. A gruesome layer of ashes and char-

coal marks the complete passing away of the Early Bronze
Age and the introduction of the Middle Bronze Age. The
great, strong, coarse pottery of the Early Bronze Age gives
way to the lighter and much more handsome pottery of the
Middle Bronze Age as clearly as the early pottery of Europe
has been displaced by Limoges and Delft ware. This change
took place at Kirjath-sepher about 1800 B. C. Those who
burned this early gateway also besieged the walls and built
fires against them which blazed up and blackened the lower
and middle courses, and left below the thin stratum of material around the foot of the wall.

Now followed somewhat rapidly two different periods of
building in the Middle Bronze Age at the east gate. What
was the occasion of rebuilding and who was the cause of it,
does not appear. Like the remains of the first building operations, there is here also at the east gate only the lowest por-
tions of the foundations. Yet in the slightly different alignment of the walls the history is plainly written. Now also
the Kirjath-sepherites set to work to make their city impregnable. Against the perpendicular wall they cast the great
sloping heap of soil and clay beaten down, extending out
about fifteen feet from the bottom of the wall and sloping up
by a convex surface to a point on the wall about twenty feet
high. This clay wall thus heaped against the stone wall they
now covered with the strong stone Canaanite revetment
wall. This revetment was not only convex on the surface, but
also extended along, as we have seen, in a series of curves so
that an enfilading fire of arrows and slingstones could be directed upon almost every point.

What a magnificent sight this wall must have been when in
a complete state! Such was the wall that confronted the spies,
if they came this way — or confronted them somewhere else,
if they did not come this way — and called forth from them
the frightened exclamation, that the cities were "walled up to
heaven." Verily, as one approaches this mountain top today
from north or south, the skyline seems to rest right upon the
top of it all around. To take such a city was a Herculean
task. No wonder it is said that Joshua and the whole army
of Israel went up to Kirjath-sepher and took it. No wonder,
either, that Caleb, in seeking to find an officer who could com-

mand at the taking of such a city of the ancient world offered such a prize.[7]

But the city was taken; the evidences of the great disaster that overtook the city, when assaulted by Othniel, are everywhere — in the debris within the city walls, about the ancient shrines which the Israelites threw down, and especially at the great gateway on the east. That thick stratum of ashes appears at a certain level, below which everything is Canaanite, *above it everything is Israelite*. After burning the city gates, throwing down the shrines and completely vanquishing the city, the Israelites began to rebuild it. At least two periods of building by them are clearly to be seen, but whether it was from destruction or from some other reason one may only surmise. It may indeed be that Cushan-rishathaim, whom Othniel as Judge defeated when he delivered Israel, burned in part at least Othniel's city, Debir, before he was finally driven off in defeat. Or it is quite as possible, if not certain, that Shishak, who devastated the fenced cities of Judah, included this old fortress among his victories. It is significant that the last building seems to have been somewhere about the time of Rehoboam and Jeroboam and Shishak.

Now for a long time, three times as long as the American Republic has lived, Kirjath-sepher seems to have continued in prosperity and greatness. The shrines were built over, in part at least upon their exact old sites, and the sacred pillars re-used for other buildings. Was there a superstitious awe of them or of disturbing them, or did the householder to whom the site belonged simply accommodate himself to stones *in situ?* At any rate, these stones were largely re-used in buildings exactly where they had stood and the rooms were arranged to follow the lines thus formed.

During all the play and counterplay of Assyrian and Egyptian invaders, Kirjath-sepher, so far to the one side of the direct line of march, remained unsubdued, indeed unassailed. Then at last came the dreadful day of doom. That ruthless troubler of the nations, Nebuchadnezzar, not satisfied with the devastation of the capital city, swept down upon these walled cities of Judah, resolved to leave the hapless people of this

---

[7] *Joshua* 10:38–39; 15:13–19; *Judges* 1:12.

unhappy land no opportunity ever again to raise the head of rebellion, razed the fenced cities of this southland and among them this great fortress of Kirjath-sepher. So great was the desolation he left behind him that from that day these cities were not again occupied for twelve hundred years. From the Early Iron Age, 600 B. C., until Byzantine times, 600 A. D., no traces of civilization have been left here. Neither Greeks nor Maccabeans nor Romans seriously built here, and even in Byzantine times there was but a farmer's occupation of the site of Kirjath-sepher.

But it is of the tragic story of these gates and walls that we are now thinking. Those were dreadful days for Kirjath-sepher. The great heaps of ashes and calcined limestones from the walls of the gateway and the evidence of the terrific heat in the passageway and from the upper structure burning and falling down into it testify to the fierceness of the struggle at that point. Yet Nebuchadnezzar does not seem to have broken in here. It was rather at the great west gate, now so utterly demolished that little more than a hole where it was remains near the surface to tell of the gate that once was. Only as we dig far into the debris do we find evidence of that structure. The great city had fallen, and now only in the twentieth century have those come who lay before the world once again its ancient greatness.

A large water tank in the tower at the east side of the entrance at the east gate was our next surprise. The tank had a cement floor and cement sides and was about eight feet square and probably of about the same depth. To this tank a stone pipe led. The pipe was made up of large stones, each with a hole about three inches in diameter through it. The way in which the stones were joined so as not to lose the water is not yet apparent.

In summing up the results of the first campaign we must gather into one picture the whole tragic story of the walls and gates. In what seems to us the dawn of history, the great Pharaohs of the Twelfth Dynasty of Egypt sat on the throne. The marvelous civilization of that land had already reached its zenith, perhaps had passed it, for the finest works of art, the most stupendous monuments of engineering, the

greatest advance in letters were already attained. The Ur
Dynasty of Babylonia, of which we are learning so much recently from the excavations of the University of Pennsylvania,
and the British Museum, was in the day of its might and glory.
The Hittites were emerging from the shadows out of which
they appear to us, however they may have appeared to the
ancient world.

It was about the time that the lonely figure Abram stalked
out into history to leave behind him such a trail of events, of
civilization, and of religion. He had set his face toward the
land of the Amorites. This is the land called Palestine now
and even before the time of Christ, so named for that mysterious people, the Philistines, who came out of mystery and
went out into mystery and left very little behind them but their
name to the land. The rest of the world lay in the obscurity
of the unknown.

The south land, at least, in Palestine of that time was, like
the feudal Europe of the Middle Ages, divided up into little
monarchies, each with its royal city and its kinglet; and sometimes at least, these rose to the dignity of kings and of strong-
holds. At this time a few people, a village perhaps or a small
city, occupied the top of an isolated conical hill which over-
hung a beautiful valley to the north and looked away to another beautiful valley and faraway hills to the south. The site
was most commanding, and easily fortified, and admirably
located for the strategic movement of armies. They called
the city Kirjath-sepher, at least in later Canaanite times, and
it rapidly grew to that greatness and importance which excites
jealousy and increases danger. They resolved to build a wall
and grow to real greatness. So they built it high and broad
and strong; they built as only the Canaanites knew how to
build with rough uncut stone, so locked and interlocked that
neither earthquake nor enemy could dislodge a stone except
by the greatest violence. At least thirty feet high they built it,
and ten feet thick on the steep side. Solid on the face they
made it of these irregular stones, but mixed with clay within.
And when the rubbish of the ages is cleared away it still
stands there in its rugged strength and greatness. Behind this
wall they felt safe.

SOME INTERLUDES

The Congress of Archæologists at its meeting in the Near East has come and gone — it has now passed on to archæological history. It was not a *"talkfest"* but a kind of *"Rundreise,"* not wholly a discussion of recondite and remote subjects, but rather an enthusiastic visit to holy places and old ruins, which are also holy places to the scientist.

From the standpoint of the individual delegate it was a great success; it was a first opportunity for many to see Bible lands, and for nearly all to see each other. And when all is said, the principle value of conventions is the value of personal contacts. Is not the same true of the whole course of one's education? From the standpoint of the Congress as a gathering it must be confessed that a convention in seven languages is rather a "howling success"; exactly so. The few who speak six or séven languages are delighted. It must be a joy and a mastery to speak understandingly and easily with all comers, "each in his own tongue in which he was born." But to one who, like the famous Max Muller, claimed to speak only English, it is most confusing. After attending the sessions of the Congress and a reception given to delegates and members at the High Commissioner's palace, one's ideas of words is so confused that he can hardly speak his own language correctly.

The personnel of the Congress was most interesting. Introduction of a few of the members will be welcomed. That sprightly little bent figure with the dark grey beard and pointed chin is Professor Sayce, so well known to the Biblical world, the genial friend of everybody and the kindly patron of every young scholar struggling upward. This vivacious figure in the white cloak and cowl, who speaks French so delightfully and has a smile for everyone, is Père Vincent; and the big, bluff, hearty white-robed monk, is Père Dhorme who presides with such grace and dignity and eloquence over the Congress. That tall, lean gentleman, with the sallow complexion and truly American look is Professor McCurdy, the paleontologist of Yale University; and this genial, lovable, smooth-faced American is Professor Dougherty, the newly-elected successor of the lamented Professor Clay at Yale. The short elderly gentleman with the florid complexion and bluff mustache is Professor Kennedy of Edinburgh University. That tall, athletic looking gentleman with flashing eyes and broad Dutch smile is Professor Noordtzij of Utrecht, Holland. The man with full dark beard, noticeable because so few young men wear full beards, is Professor Garstang, Director of the Palestine Department of Antiquities; and the other tall young man, with boyish face and bald head, is Dr. Albright, Director of the American School of Oriental Research at Jerusalem and my colleague in the excavations at Kirjath-sepher.

The Congress was opened by the High Commissioner with a sad and dramatic announcement, while all stood in hushed silence. The announcement was of the tragic death of Father Orfali, of the Franciscans, one of the men of Palestine who perhaps more than any other, has contributed to the era of good-will among the schools and sects of this age-long seat of wrangling.

A number of important announcements were either made in the sessions of the Congress or were circulated among the members. Never perhaps were so many important works of discovery under way at one time in this land. Dean Badè of the Pacific School of Religion is uncovering early Canaanite history at *Tell en-Nasbeh,* north of Jerusalem near Ramallah; the place is not yet certainly identified, but everywhere old Canaanite building is massive and impressive, and *Tell en-Nasbeh* is no exception. It furnishes another illustration of the gigantic task of the Israelites in taking the fenced cities of the land. The work at Megiddo is still only beginning, but Professor Sellin of Berlin is doing an extensive work of exploration at *Balata,* old Shechem. A visit to him and his corps of scholars and some 220 workmen was most cheering. He is doing a piece of work there especially interesting to those who love to see the early stories of Israelite and of patriarchal history paralleled by archæological evidence. But I must leave it to these men, each at his own place of work, to tell their own pleasing stories, which doubtless will soon be given to the public.

Lest some may think that life here is all of the dry-as-dust kind, I must record a few of the happenings of camp life at Kirjath-sepher. The novel events of every day are most interesting, sometimes startling, sometimes ludicrous, always illuminating; for here we live in Bible lands. A British officer from the Euphrates service said, "Out here we live in the

Bible." The man who doubts the trustworthiness of the Bible, and is determined to keep on doubting had best keep away from Bible lands.

Are we devoid of social life? Is everything mystery and work? Well, hardly so. As already related, a reception at the *mukhtar's* tent welcomed us to the community and to our work. Now this morning, the beginning of the feast of Ramadan which succeeds the month-long fast of Ramadan, there comes a smiling deputation of four men, two elderly, and two young men, bearing a great platter of feast bread, Arabic bread soaked in olive oil and sprinkled with sugar, to have us share in their rejoicing. Of course, we served them coffee (during the fast one may not offer them even coffee by day) and chatted with them a while. This evening we must call at the *mukhtar's* tent to pay our respects and doubtless drink another coffee or two. Next was an invitation to take lunch today in the neighboring village closest to the *tell*. How many more courtesies we may receive during the succeeding weeks we may easily estimate from our experience up to the present time. As yet we have not needed evening dress or even a tuxedo, but there are other amenities of social life here that are quite as necessary in the eyes of these simple, kindly people. Then, when the work is finished, or near the close of it, we will give them a feast, three or four good fat kids or lambs with about a bushel of cooked rice, confections, and coffee, coffee, coffee — bitter Arabic coffee and sweet Turkish coffee. Abundance of bread also, but we will probably have to give them European bread or Jewish bread. Oh, no, we do not lack for social doings, the work of the archæologist among the Arabs is not drab in hue.

All this does not represent a waste of time or a too great imposition on the digestive organs. To get the good-will of this people, or indeed of any people, we must treat them as fellows. We may not hold ourselves aloof from people whose service we desire. Men work willingly and happily for fellowmen, but not for masters. Then we are strangers here, sojourners in the land. To succeed well we must allow them to be our hosts and we must be willing to be guests in a real sense, and in turn show all the courtesies due from guests. This contributes more to our security than the soldier assigned to us by the government, though he is very faithful, or the old watchman and his watchful dog, who really do watch. The opening reception at the *mukhtar's* tent was Arabic friendship, which means assurance of safety on their part toward us as long as we respond in like fraternal spirit. Indeed the serving of coffee, "eating of salt," as the old saying has it, is, among the Arabs, in a sense a kind of sacrament, whereby fealty to each other is pledged. What a new window this Oriental idea opens for us into the meaning of the sacrament of the Lord's Supper. Why did our Lord ask us to remember him by eating and drinking? And why did the Passover, also, which preceded the institution of the Supper, consist of eating and drinking? It was the well known pledge of fealty between friend and friend, between earth and heaven, between the communicant and his Lord. If we do not go out from the sacrament of the Supper to a better fealty to our Lord, we have eaten and drunk unworthily, "not discerning the Lord's body." Every such memorial feast is another stage on the celestial way to our Father's house.

This is also a land of religious customs; we cannot help but admire the spirit of loyalty, though we do not believe in the customs nor the religion they embody. Our visitors of this morning remarked to us that "the followers of each religion should do what it commands." Our old watchman who watches over us at night, and who is seldom or never caught napping, gives the muezzin call to prayer, not from the minaret of a mosque in this case, but from some point about the camp. And he himself observes the hours of prayer, and I think some of the ceremonial washings. I fear these are about the only kind of washings he does observe! But a man who is loyal to God as he serves him is likely to be loyal also to men whom he serves.

Nature also vies with the people in making our stay in this community pleasant. The broad, fertile valleys here in the foothills which have been of such vivid green are now whitening toward the barley harvest. Soon the bright sickles will be gleaming and flashing in the sunlight. Pay day is also an interesting time. Sometimes its represents turbulence, but so far we have had only peace and pleasantness with these men. But there are others around about us who might not be so well disposed toward us, and so we do not keep much money in camp, but send to Jerusalem from time to time for

funds to meet the pay roll.   Last week it was my turn to go.
I took the soldier for a guide and walked to Dhahariyeh, six
miles across the mountains.   There we telephoned from the
police station for an automobile to take us to Jerusalem.   The
next morning I started back early, but got a car which was
out of condition, and after stopping about twenty times to fix
the engine, abandoned it.   Daud, an old friend of our explorations at Sodom, secured a guide, gave me a nice lunch, and
hired a donkey, and away we came for camp.   That cavalcade
was a sight.   The donkey was a little mouse-colored, unkempt
beast with one bobbed ear.   There were no proper stirrups,
and what there were were not within hailing distance of my
feet.   When I stepped over that little fellow and sat down,
my feet dragged on the ground.   I was sorely tried all the
way between the weariness of holding my feet up and the pain
of the pricking of the thistles so abundant along the way.   At
last we arrived amid much hilarity; the guide and the donkey
boy laughed along the way, everybody laughed at camp when
I arrived, and even the donkey he-hawed in his best style.

The next day, Sabbath, was a blessed day of rest.   How
gladly we hail the beneficence of that rest, for we work very
hard.   We rest and read and meditate, and at eventide hold a
devotional period, as indeed we do every evening, but it is
more extended on the Sabbath.   A great flock of cranes fed
around us and to our astonishment one of those great cranes
of the air, an airplane from Beersheba or perhaps from Egypt,
went whirring over.   What did the real cranes think?

We rise at 5:00 and breakfast at 6:30.   The workmen begin
work at 5:00 o'clock and at 8:30 the Egyptian foreman blows
his whistle for a half hour rest, and with a shout of glee all
rush to their bundles and eat their breakfast.   Again at twelve
the whistle blows for the hour-and-a-half stop for lunch.
Work in the afternoon is till five.

This morning early we are off on the journey to Jerusalem
to replenish our larder and our exchequer.   That is to say, we
planned to go early, but, alas, the morning was so cold that
our engine would not give a hoot, only a little suggestion.

Then the watchman and the cook's helper, and a visiting
Arab and the President of the staff complied with the Swiss
diligence requirement for third class passengers to "get out
and push."   By the time we reached the foot of the hill, all

went merrily. We thought we knew the camel trail to the Beersheba road, but it is astonishing how different a road looks when traveled in the opposite direction, as every wrong-doer finds in the day of repentance. When going out we found a number of roads leading off that we had not noticed, when coming in. We missed the way! A half hour gone. Then, when we reached Hebron, horrors! the whole roadway was filled with a Neby Musa parade and the onlookers. It be-comes Christians to "go softly" in a Hebron crowd, so that there was nothing for us, but to wait till the policeman gave us the signal to proceed. Another half hour gone. When we reached Jerusalem late we found three holidays in a row! Jerusalem is cursed with holidays, even with some which they call holydays. Such are the varied experiences of an archæol-ogist's career. It is not all green oases of discovery; it is largely long, sometimes weary, stretches between green spots.

Jerusalem was full of the Easter excitement which so attracts and enthralls tourists, as though it were a real part of the Holy Land of our Lord. I have been in Jerusalem a num-ber of times at Easter, but have never gone to the Church of the Holy Sepulchre at that time. I do not understand the service well and the more I understand it the less I like it. Then there is very apt to be a riot, and I am not anxious to be the "innocent bystander" who so often gets hurt. Such ritual experiences are futile, for this spectacular display is an excres-cence on the Holy Land of our Lord. It simply did not exist in his day, and gives no useful service now toward understand-ing the land of the Word. The fact is that a very large part of the things upon which tourists spend their time here wastes time that ought to be spent in reconstructing, in the imagina-tion, the Land of our Lord as it is represented by the hills and the valleys and the roads, the fields and the flowers and the customs. So we bought our supplies, worshipped on the Sab-bath, and came back to camp on Monday.

A CAVE AND RUMBLINGS OF A RIOT

There were rumors of a cave near the east gate. It is a land of caves; there was nothing surprising that the pick should reveal some cavern among the ledges of rocks that underlie the city. This would probably be no more than a hole in the ground like a hundred other holes in which the people live

around about us. The Horites are still in the land. People
who try to understand cave dwellers as surely very ancient
and primitive people will need to revise their anthropology.
Our butter and our leben come from cave dwellers; our bread
is baked by cave dwellers; our laundry work is done by cave
dwellers, there are very few people in all this part of the territory of Judah who live in what we call houses. They are
cave dwellers.

But the rumor grew from a cave to a "big cave," and possi-
bilities of a secret storage place of the city sent a thrill through
the members of the staff, and the effect among the workmen
was nothing short of a real sensation. They never can get
entirely rid of the idea that these archæologists are seeking
treasure: the idea, that we should come here and spend good
money to find a lot of old potsherds and broken down walls,
and the ruin of houses, is to them the height of absurdity.
They believe nothing of the sort. As a peasant of Dhahariyeh expressed it, "These Europeans are seeking money and
they have found a lot of it. The Europeans know just where
to look for money." So now the workmen thought, "They
have come at last to the hid treasure."

There was great and growing excitement; feverishly the
men worked to enlarge the opening that they might enter the
cave. A great stone fell down and choked the entrance, but
a sledge and many mighty blows pulverized this rock bit by
bit until at last it was deemed possible to enter, at least to
squeeze in. Then candles were brought and preparation made
for exploration, and a rope for possible emergencies, if anybody fell into a pit. Two or three of the Arabs, including the
old man who found the opening of the cave, were allowed to
enter first, that they might not suspect us of finding and
appropriating the "treasure." Behind these crept in two of
the staff and all soon disappeared and their voices died away.
They were gone a long time, so long that I began to fear they
had fallen into a pit, or lost their way in a labyrinth. At last
their voices were heard again and presently they emerged, —
about the most excited crowd I have ever seen. They were
grimy and disheveled from creeping on hands and knees and
were perspiring like politicians on election day. Even the
members of the staff were so excited they could hardly talk
coherently. "The biggest thing ever!" "No end to the

grotto!" "A great underground labyrinth of corridors and rooms!" And the old bandit who found the mouth of the cavern, for he is an ex-bandit and we were not sure that he was entirely ex-, nearly lost control of himself and dropped the ex-. He made some very bandit-like remarks. We did not consider them dangerous, but they were ominous; they showed that "the old man of sin" was very strong in him yet, if only the restraints of civilization were removd. He was about like an ex-cannibal might be supposed to be who smelled a cannibal feast cooking. This old man saw visions of countless treasure flitting through his mind, *if we could somehow be gotten out of the way.*

The next day or so as the entrance was enlarged a bit, another examination of the grotto was made more soberly, the Arabs still going ahead. Even our old bandit quieted down and lost most of his exuberance, since he did not see any heaps of gold or catch us secreting treasure. But while the first excitement was exaggerated, the real facts were startling enough. Here, just about fifteen feet below the city, was a great storage place for grain and water where these supplies might be secreted for times of siege. The stone water pipe to the tower at the gate was traced to a point over this grotto. Enclosures manifestly for the heaping up of grain were found in the rooms of the grotto. The mouths of great cisterns yawned. The corridors were traced in several directions for forty or fifty meters and then were so choked up that we could not with safety proceed.

Indeed, the corridors and rooms were almost completely choked up with soil which had been *carried in* for the purpose of filling up the place. At first we supposed the place had been choked up by the falling of chips from the scaly roof of the grotto, but it was soon evident that it was not so. The debris was not at all such material as the stone roof could supply, but fine soil from without. It had been brought in, but whether by the people of the city to choke up the place against an enemy or by an enemy to render even this part of the city forever useless, we could not know. If the inhabitants did it, then we may expect rich finds of antiquities carried in here in an effort to escape the enemy. We will not find the "treasure" the Arabs expect, for money in our sense of the term was then unknown, though it is not impossible that treasure by weight may appear. We hope not, for it means wrangling and trouble among the workmen, and we must give them the full value of the treasure for the find.

We set about clearing out the rubbish. The pottery found near the place where we broke in, which seemed a natural cavern, was mainly Israelite, i. e., of the Iron Age, or perhaps late Canaanite about the beginning of the Iron Age; but later much Bronze Age pottery was found, and as the clearing out goes on, the tendency seems to be toward the earlier periods of the history of the city. In fact the place was but little used after Canaanite times.

It is well-known that these ancient fenced cities were obliged to provide a secret water supply accessible within the city, but not accessible without. It was so at Jerusalem; it was so at Gezer. Indeed, no such walled city could hold out long in time of siege without a living spring accessible within the walls which could not be choked up by the enemy. All the water in this community is far underground. It is fifty feet to the water in the "upper and the nether springs" or wells, of Kirjath-sepher. There are no springs which come out on the surface anywhere in this region; deep wells must be made in order to reach living water. Opposite the city at a short distance across the narrow east valley is a very green and fertile spot in which are many fig and other trees. Without doubt there is water down underneath that spot, though it nowhere comes to the surface. This grotto under the city lies exactly opposite, and at a point within the city nearest to, this green spot. It is to be expected that somewhere in the grotto is a secret passage leading down to the water so that the city would have a perennial supply of fresh water, and water that could not be shut off by the enemy.

Later in the excavations, when the work of uncovering the west gate had progressed nearly to completion, the great tower, or fortress, on the north side of the gate was found to contain a room in the bottom of which was an entrance to another grotto. Around the mouth the fury of the assault of Nebuchadnezzar had so raged that the whole room had been filled with fire, a terrible burning. Indeed, the burning at this point left more evidence than perhaps at any other point around the walls and gates. This grotto was evidently first a natural cave, afterward much enlarged by excavation. Like

Upper: **THE STAFF, 1928**
Left to right, Montgomery, Gad, Schmidt, Albright, Père Vincent,
Kyle, Culley

Lower: WORKMEN AND TOOLS

(Text on page 65)

PLATE IV

the cave at the east gate, it consisted of corridors and rooms for storage. It also was so choked up that it was impossible to determine the whole extent of it. Cisterns yawned here also, and this place, equally with the grotto at the east gate, was a part of the city's defenses in times of siege. Possibly the two grottos were connected.

These two great underground defenses add another striking evidence of the engineering knowledge and skill of both the Canaanites and the Israelites who followed them. This attests once more that which is everywhere manifest here at Kirjath-sepher, that the civilization of all that period from 2000 B. C. to the days of Nebuchadnezzar was of a much higher order than has ever been claimed by those who have believed in the culture of that age; and it completely refutes beyond redemption the theory that the Patriarchal and early Israelite age was of a very low culture out of which nothing is to be expected until after a long period of development. This is the confident and ever-deepening conviction of nearly every one who does research work in the Bible lands.

As during this 1926 campaign there was but little beginning of excavation in the houses of the city, a beginning which was carried on extensively in the 1928 campaign, the whole account of that work will best be described in that next campaign, and so in the next chapter.

PART II

CAMPAIGN OF 1928

CHAPTER III

THE CITY OF THE KINGS OF JUDAH

The Industrial Age, Level "A"

Camp *Tell Beit Mirsim.*

THE Staff of 1928 consisted of the President and the Director, as in 1926, and in addition to these leaders was Professor Robert N. Montgomery of Pittsburgh Seminary, Dr. Aage Schmidt, assistant director of the Danish Shiloh expedition, Dr. Paul Culley, a missionary physician in the Philippine Islands who now ministered to the staff as well as to the whole community, and Mr. William Gad, our Egyptian surveyor. Besides these active members of the staff there was, as always in our work, Dr. C. S. Fisher as a consulting member. He was not often in camp, but his advice was always available, as was that of Père Vincent, and also Major Richmond, Director of the Palestine Department of Antiquities.

Our *hakim*, Dr. Culley, soon acquired quite a practice. These people here are themselves very helpless in sickness. At once, when it was noised abroad that there was a *hakim* in camp, they began coming from far and near at all times of the day. One man came two days' journey (two days for an invalid) to be treated. Most cases are camel bites, some of them horrible. But the people old and young are very stoical; they endure with great patience. This fortitude is very common among simple, primitive people. We develop "nerves" with culture.

Our experience here illustrates the fame of the Great Physician to whom multitudes came from afar. Now, as then, is illustrated the great physical blessings which have come to the world with Christianity, or in its wake. Heathenism, and Mohammedanism, and even Judaism, never of themselves developed scientific medicine. The highest product was Hippocrates and Galen, who could hardly pass any state medical examining board now anywhere in the

civilized world. Empirical remedies have been discovered
all over the world and much superstition has been allowed
to accumulate around them. Both heathen and Mohammedan people and especially Jews have adopted scientific
medicine and made great progress, but nowhere have they
themselves developed it aside from contact with Christian
lands.

Dr. Schmidt of the staff did a most important work at
Shiloh, the site of the Tabernacle. That place was for long
forgotten, or at least overlooked. Since it never was a town
of much importance, or for a long period, it did not leave
much of a *tell* for excavation. Thus even in the later years
of much investigation, other more promising sites were first
selected for examination. Few have been disposed to examine this one seriously.

Now Jeremiah used Shiloh as a tragic warning to Jerusalem. If the people of that city did not repent and mend
their ungodly ways, the holy city would become "as Shiloh."
At last, since the science of pottery in Palestine was developed, examination of the site was made. Dr. Schmidt
reports a most interesting set of facts. On the surface of
the ruins there was Arabic pottery, as was to be expected,
dating back possibly to about A. D. 700. Below this was
Byzantine pottery back to about A. D. 300. Below this was
found immediately the remains of the Early Iron Age I
(1200—900 B. C.). This would be from the entrance of the
Israelites into the land up to the time that Shiloh was abandoned—about the end of Samuel's life. This great break in
the evidence of culture, from the time of Samuel to A. D.
300, is a most significant fact. It can only mean that there
was no occupation of the site of Shiloh from the departure
of the Ark of the Covenant until about A. D. 300, exactly in
accord with the warning that Jeremiah gave even in his day.

THE *Tell* ONCE MORE

The *tell* presents a very busy scene, seventy-eight men
and boys all digging and scraping and carrying. Near the
center of the group, Ahmed, our tall, dignified Egyptian
foreman, stands with his little walking stick in hand, and
his sharp eyes noting every workman and every part of the
work as it progresses. Our surveyor with his plane table

set near the center also is plotting and recording every line and angle and elevation; while the rest of us watch everything that comes out, Director Albright records the finds in our folio record book, and I write about them for those who are interested to read.

Breaks and irregularity in the daily routine come by reason of our transacting our business in Jerusalem, nearly seventy miles away by the roundabout route that the automobile must go. Going to Jerusalem and returning to camp thus occupies a large place in the weeks. Added to this is the entertainment of visitors, *mukhtars,* distinguished gentlemen of the community round about us who must be treated with courtesy—Oriental courtesy—which consumes much time as well as coffee, besides the exhibition of the discoveries to visitors scientific and otherwise who come to see what has been found.

The story of all the visits would be superfluous and wearisome, but one, a few days since, is of great interest to all who read this story, as well as to us who live it. Père Vincent, the great expert on Palestinian culture, paid us a visit of a whole day, and inspected our work and considered our conclusions with his usual thoroughness. It will be as gratifying to readers as it is to us to know that he fully concurred in our interpretation of the various finds and of the exact corroboration which is here given to the historical records in the Word. He even showed us some things which we had missed. He was most enthusiastic over the contribution that this place is making to the progress of knowledge of the life and culture of Bible Lands.

INDUSTRIAL LIFE

The industrial development of this period under the kings of Judah has been a continual surprise. In the beginning of the excavation in 1926 we had found a large textile mill with dyehouse and water supply, the factory system complete twenty-five hundred years before the industrial revolution in England! If civilization runs in cycles, as some have thought, then one cycle seems to have run its course and passed away long enough to be forgotten before the introduction of the factory system in the last century. This progress in textile manufacture observed in the small excavation we were able to make in the houses in 1926 has been confirmed in the excavations of 1928. Nearly every room cleared in this large cross section of this city furnished from a score to nearly a hundred loom-weights. It is evident that the factory system was as yet combined with the general oriental method of individual workshops in the homes.

The first week of our work has given us, we find, a truly epoch-making discovery, the certain existence of the dyeing industry in ancient Israel. We found two years ago that dyehouse in connection with an extensive weaving establishment. The significance of that discovery is now fully confirmed, *it was nothing unusual.* For here is, on the opposite side of the city, a larger and more elaborate dyeing plant and round about in the rubbish of the building are very many loom-weights. Probably the weaving was done in a second or third story,—as the remains of such brick structures are abundant,—and the dyeing was done on the ground floor. It has been generally thought up to this time that no real dyeing industry existed in Israel, but that the people depended on others, especially Tyrians, and other Phœnicians, for dyeing. So to the known industrial life of ancient Israel, from 900 onward, must be added from this second campaign this industry also. Little by little the picture is being completed.

Constantly we have driven in upon us the clinging persistence of customs and methods in this land. When the dyehouses were well uncovered and the design apparent, our workmen exclaimed, "Why, this is just like the dyehouses in Hebron." In all Occidental lands, but especially in America, people are inclined to try any new and promising way of doing things. Not so here.

When lecturing in America, I am often asked, "How did these cities become filled up in the fashion of the *tells?*" It came about from the peculiar fact that the Canaanite and Israelite cities had no street-cleaning department. Not only was the rubbish of the streets allowed to accumulate, but the rubbish of the houses also was swept into the streets and left there. If the accumulation rose above the threshold,—well, they put in a new floor and raised the roof, if necessary. But *they did not clear the streets.* This reasonable explanation has now absolute physical confirmation in

Upper: ASTARTE FIGURINES FROM "A" LEVEL
Center: PALETTES FOR GRINDING COSMETICS
Lower: JUGLETS FROM "A" LEVEL

(Text on page 75)

PLATE V

Upper: TWO TYPICAL "A" LEVEL HOUSES
Lower: GRAIN PITS OF "B" LEVEL
(Text on page 99)

PLATE VI

our work this year. There are very few streets; the distinctly fortress character of Kirjath-sepher precluded the
use of much space in that way and partly the absence of
streets, especially near the gate, made the defense of the
city easier, or to put it the other way about, the possession
of the city by an enemy, more difficult. What streets there
are are "strait and narrow" ways in very fact. One such
leads up from near the east gate toward the center of the
city. When this street and the abutting houses were cleared,
the pavement of the street was clearly a foot higher than
the floor of the houses opening on it, revealing thus exactly
the process which I have described. Along another street
the house floors were as much as four feet lower.

Streets and Houses of Kirjath-sepher

Interesting things pass our camp; the novelists of the day
would call them "intriguing" things, I suppose. A donkey
and colt have just gone down the road; the serio-comic
expression on the little donkey's face—"It is to laugh." It
reminded me of the camel with all his supercilious gro-
tesquery of countenance, which needs only a lorgnette to
complete its expression of contempt. Certainly also a donkey colt is in the same class, only substituting drollery for
superciliousness. If that does not seem archæological, I
will remind the reader that this is an account of the streets
and houses of Kirjath-sepher. We have just looked upon
one of the daily scenes of those streets. That little donkey
is needed on the streets, which I would describe today, to
give the last touch of realism.

Perhaps a more technical title for this account would be
"City Planning at Kirjath-sepher." But we are not yet
ready to write upon the street plan of the city; we have
seen, as yet, too small a portion of the area of the city, only
about 4,000 square meters being uncovered this year. Yet
this small area does certainly give a very correct idea of the
general character of the streets and houses here. The plan
of the city is like the more recent, but not less classical, city
of Boston, whose streets follow the footpaths—yet not made
by the cows in this case, but by *the donkey and her colt*.

This area of 4,000 meters has now been cleared of its
debris down to the bottom of the level of Early Iron Age II,

900 B. C. This is denominated stratum "A." The streets and houses and walls and pillars are nearly all *in situ* for the lower parts of the houses; the upper parts are all burned or broken down. People not accustomed to examining archæological sites are apt to exclaim, "Well, this was certainly a rude and crude, ungainly city whose streets are twisted about and whose houses leaned every way." I suppose the streets, of course, have not been displaced in any way, but such an opinion of the houses is formed from a very mistaken imagination. Unconsciously it has compared these walls with *houses* of the present time, instead of with a *ruin* of a house burned in violence a hundred or perhaps, as in this case, three thousand years ago, and subjected to weather conditions ever since.

These houses were destroyed in a terrific conflagration. The second, perhaps a third story, made of brick, was completely destroyed and tumbled down into the first story. The plaster of the walls was almost wholly destroyed, and the cement, or plaster, floors largely ruined also. The heavy walls, however, still stand up about to the top of the great supporting pillars for the story above. And most of these pillars, partly Canaanite sacred pillars reused, are still in place. In some cases they were broken, or not a sufficient number of them was available, and Israelite pillars, roughly squared, were used; the Canaanite pillars were always hammered and rounded.

I have been photographing all the remains of the city thus far exposed this year. I worked with the assistance of one of the workmen excused by the foreman for that purpose. He was our policeman a part of the time in 1926, rather a fine looking man of average size to give in each picture a standard of comparison. I worked away until the film in the camera was exhausted—and I was approaching the same condition in the blazing hot sun. I have retreated to the tent to enjoy the rising breeze as the sun moves toward the west, and to describe the city as I see it.

The portion of the city which we have uncovered this year lies contiguous to the great east gate, south and west of the gate. The great fourteen-foot wall of the city lies alongside our excavation. Inside that wall was found one of the most elaborate systems of casemates, small rooms, and narrow passageways with no outlet, or at best only at one end in a few of them. Such formed a cul-de-sac. These casemates were first of all for serving the fighting men on the wall with food and with slingstones and arrows, boiling water and boiling oil, and all the other then known fiendish methods of maiming and killing people—almost as fiendish as the latest devices of war. These same casemates would prove traps for the enemy. If he succeeded in getting over the wall, he would drop into one of these little rooms without exit, or into a long narrow passage which would turn out to be a trap from which retreat would be cut off.

From this line of casemates, three streets ran up into the portion of the city which we have uncovered. The first of these started from the gate and was short and rough and irregular, indeed, not much more than an open place in front of the gate. The second of these streets ran due north and may be called, since we do not know its name, the Street of the Fortifications. It rose at the north end by the short flight of steps to Central Street. This wide street (about ten feet) ran east and west, except it curved around to the north at the eastern end and ran into the Dyers' Street on which the dyehouses were located. This Dyers' Street then goes west about parallel with Central Street.

These streets are nearly always above the floor levels, usually in stratum "A" nearly four feet higher, though in some few places, as we have seen, only about a foot. This sets visibly before us the way in which the *tell*, or mound on which the city stands, grew higher and higher. The streets, never cleaned, were repaved at a higher level. Again we have today an illustration of the persistence of custom in this land, for, they will go around a stone in the way for a lifetime, and none of those troubled by it would ever think of putting it out of the way. In fact they do not meddle with this old world too much; "God made it so, and so it shall be allowed to remain." If it is inconvenient, "Never mind." So these streets grew higher and higher, and, when the city was destroyed, it was rebuilt upon the higher level, and thus this great *tell* grew to such proportions.

In the center of the portion of the city thus far cleared, at the side of Center Street and about eight rods from the east gate is a little open square, a plaza. Almost in the center of this plaza is a very deep cistern, about twenty-five feet in fact, going down into the solid rock beneath the city. The upper part is like the neck of a bottle reaching down through the debris. A large flat stone covers the cistern. The hole for drawing water is quite small, scarcely more than two feet.

Round about this square the houses are ranged. The rooms are of various sizes. The most pretentious house yet found lies next to the casemates along the south wall. It consists of a large room about twenty-five feet square with seven smaller rooms. In the large room is a row of great pillars supporting the second, and perhaps a third story. These pillars are placed a little to one side of the center of the room. The smaller portion of the room seems to have been a kitchen or dining room. It has an elevated place in one corner which might serve either as a cooking place or a buffet; a small closet was at the side of it. Adjoining this large living room were smaller rooms, probably sleeping quarters, communicating with the large room usually by a door; in one instance by a wide opening with a pillar in the center of it. This house seemed to consist of six, possibly of eight rooms. It was quite as commodious as many of the less expensive of our city houses or apartments.

In the houses some great stone rollers were found, used for rolling the flat roofs. I would like to have one of them for a lawn-roller—but I do not like to "pay the freight," and that is not slang in this case. Weaving seems to have been done in every home; this only can account for the immense number of loom weights already mentioned, as coming from every house and practically nearly every room in each house. No remains of iron parts for the looms have yet come to light. Instead, we were surprised to find today in a city house two very shapely sickles. Both of them were broken, but one is quite complete except for the wooden handle. The rivets which held it in place are still in the iron. It is another illustration of the persistence of things Oriental to notice that these sickles are so exactly like the sickles used in the neighborhood now. The shape is the same, but these are a little broader in the blade, really better sickles. These sickles were used in the fields of Kirjath-sepher in the days of Hezekiah and within a few weeks the farmers round about us will be cutting the grain with sickles so like these.

Last night was the coldest night we have had and today is the hottest day. Such are the violent climatic changes here against which we must carefully protect ourselves. We have to supply ourselves with a varied wardrobe or garments of different weights, and change very frequently, sometimes two or three times during the course of one day. I came in from photographing the work on the *tell* very hot, but did not dare to throw off my coat or change it for a lighter one until in the tent I first slowly cooled off, lest a chill and illness follow.

WATER SUPPLY

Another element in the culture of this period was the arrangement for a water supply. The source of water supply is always of prime interest at the site of any ancient city, for water is a prime necessity. It is probable that there was here a secret water supply from some hidden source, as we have seen, but we have not yet located it. However that may be, it is certain that there was a large dependence upon cisterns. Two great cisterns were found in this cross section of the city. At the side of the chariot street through the center of this section, which we have named Center Street, was the small plaza about twenty-five feet square in the center of which was the large curbstone having a hole in it. It covered indeed a great cistern. This cistern we cleared in many days' work. It had at the top a long shaft, well walled and plastered, leading down to the real mouth of the cistern. The cistern itself was thus cut in the solid rock underneath the city. It was probably, indeed, I think certainly, a very old cistern coming down from the very early Canaanite times and re-used by the successive peoples on the hill, the shaft growing deeper as the *tell* rose to higher levels. There was in the stone curb a small conical hole a few inches deep. It would be a puzzle anywhere else in the world, though here in the midst of the pottery of the time, or for that matter, of the present time, it is simple enough. It was to set the pointed waterjars in, while they were being filled from the cistern. One of the dyehouses was near this cistern. At the distance of a few rods was another great cistern which was also near two dyehouses. The first cistern was like a large fat bottle; this one was globular, about thirty-five feet in each diameter and estimated to hold about 140,000 gallons. A feature connected with each of these cisterns was rather startling in its implications. The present age considers itself creator of many, many things, and perhaps plumes itself especially on its devices for hygienic protection. Especially, great filtering plants and settling basins have been provided to insure the purity of the water supply. It is ever forced upon us in our investigation of the ancient world that we of this age are not as modern as we think we are. The hygienic arrangements at Kirjath-sepher in this period under investigation were certainly not as elaborate as at modern cities, nor would any great municipal corruption be connected with them, but they were undoubtedly in their simple way effective. At the second of these great cisterns was a settling basin into which the water from the roofs of the houses was first run before being allowed to run into the cistern. The basin was shallow; the water ran off from the top of it, and it could easily and frequently be cleared of the settlings. At the other cistern, the one on the plaza, there was an entirely different system of purifying the water. The pipe which carried the water to the cistern was open in part, a drain in fact, and it had as our surveyor's level soon discovered, a slight upward gradient toward the cistern. This gradient acted as a trap to catch and hold sediment in the water. This drain also could be frequently and easily cleared of the settlings.

Furniture, Implements and Weapons

The objects found in this last Israelite city were numerous and varied. Though none of them was strikingly novel, they altogether presented a most interesting and even vivid picture of the life and culture of the times. And, of course, here as everywhere the pottery furnishes the principal evidence now remaining, as most of the other things have perished. Wood has almost entirely rotted away; iron for the most part has left little more than a spot of rust; and even bronze in the Bronze Age is often much corroded and eaten into by the chemicals of the soil.

Of implements, most of those in use today in the country round about are found. There were chisels, hammers, sledges, sickles, plowshares, rings, chains, and oxgoads. In addition, many of the great stone rollers for rolling the flat roofs were found. The plastering of floors was also practiced; we had such floors made at our camp, and strange to our eyes the plasterers were women. Men waited on them, but the skilled work was done by women. The question of admitting women to new fields of endeavor does not trouble these people now and probably never did. They would be glad to have the women do all the work!

Of implements of war, many weapons were found: arrow heads, and javelin and spear heads. As yet, no battle axes have been found at Kirjath-sepher. Some toilet articles were found; pins, fibulæ (safety-pins) and especially palettes for grinding cosmetics. One of these had twelve little receptacles around the edge, in some of which the malachite powder was still visible. Milady had her vanity case then as now! If it is not gold, like the one found at Ur of the Chaldees, it is, indeed, handsome, carved, and decorated. What Israelite beauty once prized this bauble of vanity? And was it to her that belonged also this beautiful little Astarte figurine? Did she, and other ladies of the city of the Kings of Judah and her modern sisters of the flapper sorority, also secretly worship Astarte? The constant occurrence of these indubitable evidences of the Israelite proclivity toward idolatry gives point to the denunciatory words of judges and prophets. And how vivid are the scathing words of Isaiah, some centuries later, as we look on this bauble of some belle of Kirjath-sepher! "In that day the Lord will take away the bravery of their tinkling ornaments about their feet, and their cauls, and their round tires like the moon, the chains, and the bracelets, and the mufflers, the bonnets, and the ornaments of the legs, and the headbands, and the tablets, and the earrings, the rings, the nose jewels, the changeable suits of apparel, and the mantles, and the wimples, and the crisping pins, the glasses, and the fine linen, and the hoods, and the vails."[1] We have not got-

---

[1] *Isaiah* 3:18—23.

ten all these gewgaws from this particular maiden, but doubtless she had a good many of them.

CULT OBJECTS AND INSCRIPTIONS

No cult objects were found in this last Israelite city, except an occasional Astarte figurine. The Jews made no images themselves. But sometimes they fell into the idolatry of the people of the lands. These Astarte figurines were probably charms, mascots representing superstition rather than idolatry, much as Egyptian women of today practice the use of such charms as superstition, and not a few people in western civilization lug some mascot around. Sometimes one is terrified to think ancient Palestinian people were as superstitious as some modern Americans.

The Jews were never much given to inscriptions. A few interesting, but very short, ones were found. Quite occasionally a potsherd was found which seemed to have traces of what probably had once been ink writing, but which the dampness of the debris had absorbed until there was nothing intelligible left. There were also quite a number of jar handles found which had an impression as of a seal or of a thumb, but which was quite destitute of any lettering. The meaning of these was somewhat puzzling, but they probably indicated the beginnings of the practice of stamping jar handles, at first only with a mark, and later with a similar mark in which was a brief inscription. The whole significance of the stamped jar handles is still not quite clear. The jars bearing such stamps were all of a standard size and shape. It seems most likely that they were intended to hold the taxes paid in kind and that the stamp on the jar handle was in the nature of a receipt, at least a certification that so and so had paid his tax, attested by a clay or wax impression.

One jar was found on the side of which were plainly the letters B TH which vocalized might be "Beth," house, and so had been followed by a man's name, or the same letters might be "bath," a Hebrew measure. Most probably it was intended simply to denote the capacity of the jar. If we had all of that broken jar, we would probably have one vessel said to hold a bath.

No properly stamped jar handles of the kings of Judah

Upper: **KIRJATH-SEPHER AS OTHNIEL FOUND IT**
Lower: **A DYEHOUSE FROM THE LAST ISRAELITE CITY**
(Text on page 112)

PLATE VII

Upper: **AN IDOL OF SERPENT WORSHIP**

Center: **SMALL LIBATION TABLE**

Lower: **SCULPTURED LION**

(Text on page 122)

PLATE VIII

were found in '26 and none this year until late in the season. We had about concluded that our opinion in '26 that the city was finally destroyed by Nebuchadnezzar would have to be revised. The practice of stamping jar handles was introduced about the time of Hezekiah and so, such jar handles ought not to be found here, if Sennacherib destroyed the city and it was not rebuilt. If no such jar handles were here, then the destroyer was, indeed must have been, Sennacherib at the time when he "shut up Hezekiah like a bird in a cage," to use his own boastful expression. He then destroyed the fenced cities of Judah of which this was one. If no stamped jar handles were in this ruin, then we must conclude that the city was not rebuilt after the time of Sennacherib.

But in tracing the great chariot street up through the city from the great east gate, we found it to run alongside the north side of the cross section we were cutting down through the debris. It ran directly toward the highest point in the ruins which might reasonably be some great public buildings. While most of our workmen were clearing away the walls and floors of the city of the kings of Judah preparatory to going down to the next level, the city built by the Israelites, when they first came, and destroyed by Shishak, we set the remainder of our workmen to excavating along this chariot street toward the center of the city. It was a little experimental research to see what was in store for us in that region. We soon came upon the walls of a great house, perhaps it might be better said a strong house. It had walls four feet thick. Whether it was a palace, or a temple, or the citadel, or simply a prison, we did not learn. When the cross section was cleared we went on with our work in the systematic fashion required. Another season we will follow that chariot street. But one thing we learned in this brief investigation; we found around about that strong building a number of stamped jar handles, probably indicating that we were approaching the government houses of the city where such certified jars would be kept, and certainly indicating that Sennacherib was not the final destroyer of the city, but that it continued on to the next great destruction, that by Nebuchadnezzar. So that our first conclusion was after all correct.

Most of these jar handles contained the words, "To the King," and then the name of the pottery. One was found, however, that was quite unique. It was exquisitely done, the die had been so delicately engraved that we required a reading glass most clearly and certainly to transcribe it. The lettering was in the Phœnician alphabet, the old Hebrew alphabet in use in all that age of Palestinian history. The inscription was in two lines, manifestly arranged to be of about the same length. The upper line read, "To Eliakim," the lower, "The servant of Jochin." The word here used for servant was not *ebed* the usual word, but *naar* the unusual word which occurs in the mention of the 318 "servants" of Abraham, not ordinary servants, but rather clients, or officers or retainers, like the servants of a feudal lord in the Middle Ages. Then "Jochin" is an abbreviated form of Jehoiachin, which has other illustrations. It was here manifestly employed in order to make the lines of about the same length. The full writing of the king's name would have made the line entirely too long. We have here then a jar paid into the treasury of the lask king but one before the city was destroyed by Nebuchadnezzar, and thus certainly was Nebuchadnezzar the destroyer. This inscription reveals a high degree of artistic skill in the engraving of the die for the stamp, and as Jehoiachin reigned only three months and eight days, we have here a most exact chronological date.

Another insight into the civic life of this city is given by the discovery of an almost complete set of weights. These were found, not in any of the homes nor in a shop of some merchant, but in the tower on the north side of the west gate. Found thus in this official quarter, and being almost a complete set, and being accurately and for the most part beautifully made, these weights must have been official in character, a set of standard weights of the city government. Few laws are so difficult to enforce, or reveal more of the good intent of the government, than laws of weights and measures. We have here another indication of the high development of civic life in the culture of the time of the Kings of Judah.

Now look at these smooth, shapely, rounded objects of stone with flat bottoms to stand firmly, and so evenly graded from this tiny one the size of a large marble to this big one the size of a forty-pound round cannon shot. Occasionally one of a slightly different shape is found, as though belonging to a set of different design. These are the weights for the scales. The delicate exactness with which they are made shows unmistakably that they were standard weights; whether the official standard of the city or only made to conform with that does not matter. We may picture a merchant among his wares with his scales before him and such a collection of weights, ready to weigh out the produce, to his customers. The perfectly formed character of the weights shows his customers that they are standard weights. This is not all the little weights tell; standard weights imply an authority to fix a standard and ability to enforce it. But a government attending to such matters must have been an effective government, which did not, of course, consist of this one thing alone. Civilization and culture are like the kingdom of heaven in one respect; they spread "like leaven" in every direction. They rarely extend and develop in one direction or consist of but one good thing. A high development in one direction implies like development in other directions. So that the implication of these marvelously shaped weights is of a well-developed government that reaches out in various other directions.

I recently remarked to a company of ladies and gentlemen that the wonderful development of engineering in the defenses of Kirjath-sepher utterly refuted the theory, long advocated by many, that the Patriarchal Age was an age of nomads in this land, and that there was a very low state of culture. One instantly replied, "Oh, but there is no evidence of any deep culture." I replied that the military engineering of that age, which, here at Kirjath-sepher, employed every device known to military engineering did not and could not exist alone. People who could do such things could certainly do some other things; those of such high development in a difficult mathematical science surely were not deficient in culture in many other directions. Culture is *always* like leaven that spreads in every direction. Could anyone be so stupid as to suppose, for example, that the ancient Greeks who made such unparalleled advances in architecture had no other culture than that? Great cultural development in any one direction always implies development in other directions also.

WRITTEN ON POTSHERDS

It was customary in the days of the prophets to write on potsherds. Some of such writing, though probably by lesser dignitaries than prophets, we have found in our work here, but so weathered as to be utterly illegible.

But "written on potsherds" has also in these days a metaphorical meaning which needs illustration. So this is to be a lesson on the things "written on potsherds," that is, the information concerning Canaanite and Israelite history which archæologists glean almost wholly from broken pottery. As most popular readers of this time, or any other for that matter belong in the first-grade class in potsherds, the lesson will be simplified for all such, even at the risk of some repetition of what has been stated very briefly.

The a-b-c of archæology in Bible Lands is this literature of potsherds. It seems to most people largely guesswork, and yet it is far from being that; it is, indeed, a very exact source of information. The Periods of Archæological history in Palestine are, as we have seen, the Bronze Age; Early, Middle, and Late; and the Iron Age; I, II, and III. Each of these various Ages and the divisions of each has its own very distinctive pottery, so distinctive that it never misleads us. The lesson today will be in the Early Iron II, dating from 900 B. C. to 600 B. C. Or, as it appears to us on the mound — where we must examine from the top, the latest remains, down to the oldest at the botom — it is rather from 600 B. C., the final destruction of the city, back to 900 B. C., at the bottom of a large section from which we are removing the debris. We call it technically the "A" level.

The pottery of this period has, for the most part, a very great sameness, that is, the common pottery of this period is very common indeed, yet of good quality. But there are two kinds of pottery that very distinctly mark and distinguish all this period. There is the ring-burnished pottery[2] and the black cooking pot, though the cooking pot is found in other ages. The cooking pot was black not only from having been over the fire, but from the composition of materials in its making. It was composed of a dark clay mixed with grit or fine pebbles. The clay without the pebbles would expand

---

[2] Cf. *Annual of American Schools of Oriental Research*, Vol. XII, p. 78 ff.

and crack over the fire, but the fine pebbles, not expanding like the clay, neutralized the expansion of the clay and the pot did not crack. The invention of this pot was even a greater aid to the Canaanite and Jewish housewife than has been the invention of the fireproof glass baking dish in the modern home.

The other and chief characteristic of this Early Iron II is the ring-burnished pottery. This was beautiful, quite decorative indeed. Very simple in design to be sure, for it was but lines usually of various shades of pink and red and sometimes almost maroon running round and round the vessel. These lines were laid on a terra cotta background of various shades, and highly burnished with a pebble while the pot was still on the wheel. The burnishing was often on the inside of the pot only, though sometimes on the outside as well. Such pottery, if it were imitated today, would be very striking and probably at once become a vogue. I had often wondered, before the Tut-ankh-amen craze turned the decorators toward Egypt for designs, that they had not long before turned in that direction. It is equally a wonder that the chinaware potters of today do not turn to the ancients for new(?) and striking designs. A large banquet bowl with four flat handles in this beautiful ring-burnished ware was very common at Kirjath-sepher in this period. A great trencher of this ware which we found in 1926 and were able almost completely to reconstruct was like the "lordly dish" set before Sisera, and would grace a great banquet table anywhere today.

Matching pottery, putting together the broken fragments found in the ruins and making complete vessels, beats crossword puzzles and, among archæologists, has more fans, and more sorely obsessed also. The Field Director of our staff, Dr. Albright, is an expert, and matching pottery has so bewitched him that he was caught at the lunch table a day or two ago unconsciously trying to match fragments of orange rind!

It may seem to some that the broken pot and the potsherd in all their humbleness and, to many, such seeming worthlessness, hold too important a place in Biblical archæology. Let it be remembered that they held a not less important place in the period of the kings of Israel which this period under examination actually covers. If the potsherd sometimes served the prophet as a means of communicating his message, it is quite certain also that the humble potsherd is a very effective means in possession of the archæologist for learning and teaching the history of civilization of that same period. In these potsherds will ultimately be found the material for a real and reliable chronology of the whole Old Testament period. The most heroic, and sometimes futile, efforts have been made to estimate and construct a chronology according to our astronomical system from the materials of the Old Testament *which were not given in accord with such a system.* The result has been confusion and wrangling.

The impression which is being continually deepened by our investigations at *Tell Beit Mirsim,* and which is especially deepened by this study of pottery, is that the industrial life of Israel in the period from 900 B. C. onward to the end of the kingdom at the Exile was well developed. The evidence of weaving and dyeing, of the pottery industry, and especially engineering, is now greatly strengthened. The evidence of the weaving industry is overwhelming. Basketful after basketful of loom weights come down each day from the *tell.* The evidence of these now added to the dyehouse with four vats, all in a small area of about four thousand square meters, indicates a thriving state of this industry. It must be kept in mind also that this site was far away toward the southern frontier of Judah, over forty miles in direct line from Jerusalem and thirteen from Hebron.

The lesson in pots then is not only that the message of the pots is clear and unmistakable to the archæologist by reason of certain persistent types, but is also becoming every day a clear message like that of the prophets of old, a message to all people of the state of civilization in the land at various ages, and that message is precisely of the same import as is conveyed by the historical documents of the Word. That is to say, they have the earmarks of authenticity, and are not at all of the fictitious character given to them by the supposition that they represent culture of a much later period thrown back upon the screen of antiquity. Everywhere the trustworthiness of the ancient documents stands out.

In addition to these most distinctive marks of the Early Iron Age II, there were a number of others which may be mentioned as of quite frequent use, but of less importance. One type especially was of very frequent use and might be a principal distinctive one, except that it seems, at least to us, of rather small importance in itself. This is the little black, or very dark gray, bottle so much used by the Israelites of this period. Multitudes of them come out of the debris of the houses. They were used as ointment and perfume pots, perhaps also for coloring for the eyelids, thus occupying much the same place among Israelite women as milady's rouge jar in her boudoir. Perhaps some of the ladies will think this is to give it a very important place among the antiquities, a distinguishing place indeed. But, after all, it was a small thing in the life of the people and an unattractive piece of pottery in itself.

Then certain long-necked water flagons were found in this period, especially in the latter half of it, which are quite distinctve. Many of the large pots or amphoras— they are called by the Greek name, for lack of a better — have pointed bottoms. They were not meant to stand upon a floor or a bench or even on the ground, but only in a large hole somewhere. Sometimes a pottery ring made for the purpose was used as a stand.

POTTERY CHRONOLOGY IN BIBLE LANDS

Two things are mysteries, utter mysteries, to many Bible students and to most of those who try to understand what archæological discoveries have to do with the Bible story. These mysteries are pottery and chronology.

A few people still pin their faith to the chronology printed by some publishers in the margin of Bibles, or to some very confident assertion of a somebody that he has worked out "The final, and absolutely correct chronology of the Old Testament." Others, on the contrary, perceiving the irreconcilable differences of opinion among chronologists, give up the whole question of dates in despair and foolishly conclude that because nobody has been able to figure out the exact chronology of Old Testament events according to our way of reckoning, therefore the Bible is untrustworthy in this respect, and, as the human mind is incorrigibly disposed to be logical, that, "false in one thing, false in all"; the Bible is untrustworthy in chronology, therefore untrustworthy in all things. Ergo, not the Word of God at all!

Then, if chronology is a counsel of despair to some, when one begins to talk about pottery of the Bronze Age, pottery of the Iron Age, it all sounds to many people like the prattle of some ethnologists of the evolutionary type, who would make us believe that the progress of civilization followed an absolutely regular procedure upward through the ages, and outward through all lands. As this scheme of uniformity of development has so many breaks and eddies and relapses to contend with and seems on the whole so vague and visionary, people are apt to conclude that the talk about pottery in the history of Bible Lands comes from the same piece of evolutionary material. This pottery is also a mystery.

Now, when I set as the title of this archæological account from Kirjath-sepher, "Pottery Chronology in Bible Lands," and join these two mysteries together into one picture, I suppose some will be ready to throw up their hands in despair, and perhaps, figuratively "cast me out of the synagogue."

Well, the task I have set myself is to make one of these mysteries explain the other. I sit at this moment in my Jerusalem home amid a horrible sandstorm. It is about as much as one's eyes are worth to go out unprotected into such a storm. Probably work at the *tell* is completely suspended until the storm is over. So I will not try to go back to camp until it is possible to continue the work, but will write of these mysteries. Père Vincent, who is an expert of experts in Palestinian pottery, says that, if ultimately he cannot work out the chronology of Old Testament times from the pottery to within a half century, he will give up the study of archæology and take to raising lentils. That sounds very frivolous for a pious monk to say, but he is a witty Frenchman as well as a devout ecclesiastic, and that is only his way of declaring his absolute confidence in pottery chronology in Bible lands.

Does anybody say that "within half a century" would be very unsatisfactory? At least it would be an improvement, a great improvement, upon the chronology of the Old Testament as we now have it. While a few dates are pretty well made out, there are only a few, and that *by themselves.* When taken in connection with the whole sweep of that portion of history, they become far more vague than "within half a century." It must not be overlooked that however confidently publishers print chronological dates, when they wish to sell their books, chronologists wrangle bitterly among themselves over the date of the Exodus and of the Conquest and so, from the dominating character of these dates, all other dates along the line become almost equally uncertain. Here there is a difference and uncertainty of, not half a century, but *three whole centuries,* and some extremists would widen the breach still more.

It will be quite sufficient here to state some facts and principles which have been established.

I. Our system of chronology is epochal; the Old Testament is synchronistic. We wish always to date events B. C. or A. D. The Old Testament books knew nothing of such a system, and so did not date events in that way at all.

II. We view history always in a line of succession; the Old Testament writers viewed it in the plane of contemporaneity, usually the plane of life in which they themselves were living. If they spoke of other times, they transferred themselves to those times. They had indeed a grammatical device, the "*vav* conversive," for doing this. Their system was as correct as ours, but the difficulty of translating the one to the other is very great. Probably an exact chronology of Old Testament events according to our system cani never be made out, simply because the Old Testament writers do not supply the data for such a purpose. People talk glibly about "Biblical Chronology." Chapter and verse, please?

III. Our system of chronology is mathematical according to astronomical time reckoned by the clock and recorded in the calendar. The people of Palestine in Old Testament times, whatever they may have known of astronomy, had neither clocks nor calendars.

IV. Numbers are used by us very definitely in chronology; Old Testament numbers were often used symbolically, not only in chronology, but elsewhere. We sometimes use numbers so ourselves. I recently heard a distinguished scientist say, "There are thousands of these instances," meaning, of course, "'They are of common occurrence." So in the Old Testament "thousands" often means "many," as the "thousands of Israel." We speak of "a decade," a vague expression not meaning exactly ten years. So the Bible in the Old Testament period uses "forty years" and multiples or divisions of forty. Right proportions and correct impressions were first considerations in Old Testament chronology.

Now pottery chronology reflects very exactly these same characteristics, peculiar as they are.

I. It is not mathematical, but descriptive, symbolical, typical, as typical as the "Victorian Age" is of that phase of Anglo-Saxon life and culture.

II. It is not epochal, but synchronistic. It determines dates by resemblances of culture.

III. So it always views Old Testament history on the plane of contemporaneity, rather than in the line of succession.

Certain types of characteristics distinguish each age; wherever those characteristics are found, that age is certainly indicated. Thus the events put themselves into groups of times and localities, and may not be mingled together by any theory of growth and development. Pottery thus becomes a solvent for critical dilemmas. The pottery age reflected in the Pentateuch, or in the early or the late prophets, must reflect the culture of the times depicted, and could not be "reflected back from later times."

Thus, while pottery chronology will never give the exact year B. C. for any event, any more than the Old Testament gives such dates, it will determine it by the age of culture out of which no critical theory of any kind whatsoever, radical or conservative, can take it. Events of the Victorian Age, which reflect the customs *of that time,* might just as well be transferred by critical theory to the Middle Ages or to the Twentieth Ceutury.

But how are we to translate this pottery chronology into years and centuries? The task might at first seem to be hopeless, but it is not really so. The dates of certain events whose place is clearly indicated by the pottery chronology are also dated with comparative accuracy B. C. by means of Egyptian or other events. From these events as "ancient landmarks," the mill-stream of history may now be traced backward and forward in that right proportion which will give correct impressions. Thus a real chronology will result which cannot be perverted to the uses of mistaken theories. The efforts of all nations have been to get coinage that cannot be counterfeited. *Pottery chronology is a system of historical coinage that cannot be counterfeited.*

An outline of the main phases of the pottery chronology of Bible Lands is as follows: Strange to say, they are not named from the various kinds of pottery used, but from the various kinds of metal prevailingly used together with the pottery. So the Bronze Age pottery was not made from Bronze, as some one interpreted my lecture once, but was the pottery at the time when bronze was the metal in common use.

I. The Bronze Age, when only copper was used for metal weapons and tools. It ran from near 3,000 B. C. down to about 1200 B. C., Early Bronze, Middle Bronze, Late Bronze. This was when "the Canaanite was in the land." It also coincides in large part with the Patriarchal period in the Old Testament history. All the various phases of culture, from the time of Abraham on, harmonize exactly with the Patriarchal history.

II. The Iron Age, when iron was the principal metal used. It ran from about 1200 B. C. onward, Early Iron I, II, III. This was the Israelite period from the Conquest on to the Exile, and at the beginning, was the time of the Philistine power in the land; and after the Exile the same Iron Age continued through Greek, Maccabean, and Roman, and onward to the present time.

It may be that sometimes too much stress is laid upon pottery to the neglect of other evidences of civilization and culture, but it can hardly be over-estimated in its importance for the correct synchronizing of Biblical events in relation to other world events and dates backward and forward.

It is gratifying to us, and will be of interest to all readers, to know that this site of Kirjath-sepher is furnishing the best conspectus of pottery history and the best basis for pottery chronology that has been supplied by any one place in Palestine. It is especially valuable because here the point in history of the settlement of Israel at this place is so exactly indicated in the pottery that there cannot be any mistake. Everything below that certain layer of ashes is Canaanite and everything above that level is Israelite. Thus we have an absolutely fixed point from which to trace events and dates backward and forward. We are securing many objects of great interest and value; to the present date, I think about 400, with much of this season still before us. But altogether, aside from these, if we secured nothing from the two seasons' work and expense at Kirjath-sepher but this advance in the pottery history and chronology of Bible lands and Bible times, all the expenditure would be amply justified and we may well be satisfied.

CHAPTER IV

THE JUDGES AND THE MONARCHY

THE CULTURE OF CONQUEST DAYS, LEVEL "B"

Camp *Tell Beit Mirsim.*

IT IS in the middle of the night. A half dozen figures, wrapped from head to foot, are slumbering round about me, some on beds, some on reclining chairs, some on automobile cushions, and some on the cement floor. Fortunately none of them snore. Even rifles stand on the rack in the corner, and other military accouterments are scattered about. In fact, we are lodged in the police station! It is my first experience, but we are not prisoners, we are guests. One of the officers even offered me his bed, he himself to sleep on the floor. I would not consent to that arrangement, but the hospitality that would make the offer can be appreciated anywhere, any time.

But I must begin at the beginning of the story to find a reason for our "detention in the police station." It is all linked up with the devastating tediousness of getting things a-going in the Orient. It is the land of "never mind"; things are done "tomorrow"; some of them are sure to be forgotten today. Three Egyptians are with us, trained workmen of much experience at other excavations. Two of them had gone ahead to camp with a lorry party, one was to go with us in the automobile. He went to market, while we waited. Hoping to get started at two o'clock, it was actually 3:15 when he returned and we finally got all together and went swiftly down the Hebron road.

The weather was fine, the road excellent, and the scenery beautiful. How I love this land, and more and more year by year. All went deliriously well until — bang! The proverbial grain of sand in a shoe is as nothing to a half-inch nail in an automobile shoe. Forty minutes gone and a camel trail thirteen miles of the way yet before us, while the sun was hastening to the setting; and two new tires *forgotten and forty-five miles away.*

The lorry appeared coming back from taking down camp equipage; we requested the driver to turn and take us to camp. Then there was what the Chinese call a "talkee talkee." The precious time till sunset was rapidly passing, until at last the secret came out; he offered to take us for *two pounds.* I knew that was what was hidden under his turban, and was only surprised that he had not demanded three, or even four pounds. We agreed, and he agreed, and then he rued his bargain, probably because we had consented so readily. So he pretended that he could not find where the camel trail turned off the Hebron-Beersheba road, although he had come out of it a few minutes before, and had driven twice over it within a few hours. So we jolted off in that lorry to Dhahariyeh fifteen miles away. How I sympathize with wounded soldier boys who had to ride in those springless chariots. The outcome was the spending of the night in the police station.

Reveille was for us at 4:30. I had slept rather lightly for about seven hours. At the first break of day I rose and walked out to find the town already stirring. I waked up our sleeping company, we loaded our car with the camp equipment and again rushed down the Hebron-Beersheba road. Our supper had been a very light lunch eaten in that bouncing lorry in the darkness. Bread without butter, eggs without salt, with cheese and oranges for seasoning. Breakfast there would not be at all until we reached camp, now nearly thirty miles away, half of the way a camel trail. We found the entrance to that trail only a few rods beyond where we had broken down last evening. By half past seven we came near the camp and got such a welcome as only desert people can give. Never imagine you are not seen and known in this land even though you yourself see no one. From every direction persons were coming to welcome us, and two men hastened to show us a change in the road and pilot us near to the "nether spring." Workmen were busy building an addition to our camp, two stone houses, over which we will stretch Bedouin tent cloth of camel's, or goat's hair.

"MAIN STREET" AT KIRJATH-SEPHER

When we arrived at camp we returned into the Patriarchal Age. We are living in tents with Abraham, Isaac, and Jacob. Those may not be exactly their names, but they are all around about us living in exactly the same way as the patriarchs, and we are tenting among them. The patriarchal life around us is a constant surprise and delight. There is not only the tent life, but the cave life of the troglodytes, which preceded, and, strange to say, still continues. Within 150 yards of the camp are four cave-dwellings and within a mile, perhaps fifty. Most of them are occupied this summer, though some are "to let," only no real estate agent is necessary. Then there are some people who live in houses, or in tombs, or in the ruins of Crusader homes. Whatever the state of civilization may have been here in Greek times, and Roman times, or Byzantine and Crusader times, in these present times there is a complete lapse into patriarchal and pre-patriarchal life.

Now, we do not live quite that way; we are tenting in the midst of these people, but "Main Street" with us is a mixture of the patriarchal and the tourist ways. A broad stone wall encloses a half-acre court nearly all the way around, a stone wall, over which people may climb, but which is a hint that they should stay out. Hints, however, are not much more effective here than anywhere else. We are anxious that the workmen do not come in around our tents; they leave too many of their own fleas and do not take away any of ours! Our waiter boy stands at the eastern entrance — automobile entrance — of our court at the end of work-time and shoos them away, allowing to pass only those carrying baskets, or bringing messages, or having some other legitimate excuse for coming in. He is as active as a monkey, knows his job, and does it well.

If we take our stand outside the entrance at the eastern end of the camp and look west, an interesting scene is before us. Two large Bedouin tents of goats' hair and having stone walls underneath them are first, one on each side. In one is installed our Armenian cook with his pots and pans and brazier and gasoline burner. There he gets up wonderful meals and speaks Armenian, Kurdish, Turkish, Greek, and Arabic, and smokes a hubble-bubble. Opposite the kitchen the other Bedouin tent is used as a workshop. On the floor of it, our *Haj*, the night watchman, rolls himself up and sleeps by day. At the corner next to Main Street he has a little "fireside" where he makes a "fire of thorns" in the evening and there the *Haj* and Ahmed, the Egyptian foreman, and the cook

sit and hob-nob and smoke an evening pipe. I have introduced the members of the staff occidental fashion; the way
in which these cronies would introduce us is different. I am
the Old *Khawadjah;* Dr. Albright, the Young *Khawadjah;*
Professor Montgomery is Teacher; Dr. Culley, the *Hakim,*
and Dr. Schmidt, *el-Yehudi;* though he is a Danish Luth-
eran, they will not be persuaded that he is not a Jew. William, our Egyptian surveyor, is the Scribe.

Now going down Main Street, on one side one sees the large
dining tent and the tent of our Egyptian foreman and assistant, and on the other side the tents of *el-Yehudi* and the
Scribe. Beyond this, at the lower end of the street, are two
green tents, with awnings, where the *Khawadjahs* and the
Hakim live. A tall pole near the center beyond those tents
bears aloft our street light at night, so that the whole length
of the street is lighted up before the *Haj* our watchman.
Last of all an automobile closes the end of the street. No
limit on parking hours.

Morning comes in this clear atmosphere at *Tell Beit Mirsim,* just a little before sunrise. The first sound heard from
the tents is every man knocking his shoes against something
to dislodge any predatory scorpion which may have adopted a
new home in the night. We have never found one in a shoe,
but keep up the search. The idea of one's great toe meeting
in such a social way the sting in the tail of a scorpion is
fearful to contemplate!

About the time the face of the sun appears over the corner
of the fortress, the faces of the members of the staff are
introduced to the cool waters of the "nether spring." Our
Egyptian foreman goes by, and the workmen troop in from
every direction. Our breakfast is served at six-thirty. We
do not have anything for breakfast except oatmeal and milk
and sugar, bacon and eggs, bread and butter and peanut butter, jam or fruit, coffee, hot milk or chocolate! Not so bad
for camp among the patriarchs either.

Then we sort pottery, record the finds, survey and plot
on the *tell,* inspect the progress of the workmen, take
photographs and moving pictures, and write. Ofttimes we
eat breakfast muffled up in our overcoats, but by eleven or
twelve o'clock the atmosphere is blood heat, and the water is
blood heat. You can tell when you are getting a drink by

Upper: FURNITURE INLAY CARVED FROM BONE
Center: VEINED ALABASTRONS FROM AN "E" PALACE
Lower: GAME PIECES FROM AN "E" PALACE

(Text on page 128)

PLATE IX

Upper: **THE STAFF, 1930**
Left to Right, Kelso, Huffman, Saarisalo, Albright, Kyle, Glueck,
Sellers, Schmidt; Kneeling, Araj, Gad
Lower: ARABS WATCHING THE BEERSHEBA CIRCUS

(Text on page 138)

PLATE X

seeing the water go down in the cup rather than feeling it going down the throat. By three o'clock the breeze comes from the Mediterranean and sometimes we have to resort again to our overcoats. These violent changes make it so necessary to change our clothing two or three times a day, to avoid the diseases common in the Orient.

Lunch is a dish of meat with vegetables, and cheese, and dessert, stewed fruit or pudding. Then tea or hot milk for those who wish it. After lunch is a siesta, the length of it depends upon the heat of the day and the persistence of the flies. Once in a while a gad-fly silently inoculates one's nose or ears or cheek and leaves a lump as big as a pea and unspeakably itchy. Ammonia will stop the itching, but the lump is a permanent decoration for some days! By two o'clock all are usually awake and at work. The workmen on the *tell* have already been chanting over their tasks for nearly an hour. The afternoon passes more rapidly even than the morning. At five o'clock the foreman's whistle blows, the crowd gathers about the entrance to chatter and to get a drink, and then in little groups to ramble away to their homes at any distance from an eighth of a mile to four or five miles.

Dinner is a delicious soup served piping hot, then a dish of meat with two or three vegetables, and an excellent dessert, — at times a caramel pudding, sometimes Egyptian milk-rice, sometimes, and best of all, peaches or pears from Tasmania; with tea, coffee or chocolate. Oh, we have a good cook and give him good things to cook. The work is strenuous and the conditions of life rather hard, so that we must have nourishing food. I have never had better health. A former year we lived largely from canned food, but this year we bring fresh bread, vegetables, and fruits from Jerusalem, buy lambs and kids in the neighborhood, and eggs, — this year's eggs, too! from the farmers and their wives. An old negro collects the eggs, one or two from each home. And all the time, the Canaanites "labored and we enter into their labors," for the "nether spring," walled up before the time of Abraham, supplies us with water that does not need to be boiled.

Then evening comes with a gorgeous sunset that only a Rubens could paint or a Homer describe. The *Haj* lights his lantern and hangs it on the "lamp post." The staff has evening prayers and the *Haj* devoutly bows toward Mecca. We sit about our table after prayers for a discussion of the day's events and their significance, much archæological survey of literature, and pleasant gossip of the work in many fields of discovery. Sometimes we bend over that table until a late hour, but usually nine o'clock calls us to our couches. All is quiet until another glorious day. Practically in the open air, we sleep well. The Old *Khawadjah* is an expert at sleep, and little time is lost in any of the tents.

A Feast in a Cave

The twelfth of April closed with another feast. As we walked down the green valley near sunset, one after another of the men of the neighborhood joined us until we were a party of twenty-five or thirty, when we arrived in the village of the *mukhtar* — another of the *mukhtars* of this community — and all going to the feast. We were ushered into a wierd, romantic cave in the limestone rock. It had been swept and garnished until it seemed immaculately clean. Rugs and richly decorated cushions and couches awaited us. Coffee was served and then a delicious roast turkey dinner with all the trimmings, Arabic trimmings, in which gravy with leben took the place of cranberry sauce. It was truly patriarchal in character with perhaps the single exception of the addition of spoons. This man is a wealthy land-owner, worth about $150,000, yet he lives among the poor villagers in this primitive fashion. Wealth does not indulge itself among these people as it flaunts its luxuriousness in the Occident.

We were escorted homeward by the *mukhtar* himself for a little way, as Abram accompanied his angel guests a little way, and a number of his people all the way. A constable also accompanied us with his gun, not for protection, but for decoration of the occasion. We were "distinguished visitors" and they accorded us a military escort after the fashion of some little monarch or some great city councilman!

The daily clinic of our *Hakim* has grown to such proportions that the item of medicine has to be added to our accounts. But it is a great joy to help these poor people so helpless in their suffering. Moreover, the rendering of this unselfish service to them secures from them such gratitude as ministers to our welcome and our security.

This evening the Teacher and the Old *Khawadjah* go up to Jerusalem for supplies and for the mail. The ladies of the staff, who are our artists at Jerusalem, are planning to come down and spend one night in camp. And we are planning a surprise for them, invitation to a native feast with our *mukhtar*. In social events, that will be an experience of a lifetime.

Laying Waste the Fenced Cities of Judah

We have definitely determined that Nebuchadnezzar was once the final destroyer of Kirjath-sepher — but not now; we are. When we got down to the floor levels and the street paving of the city of Early Iron Age II, 900–600 B. C., and had measured and leveled and plotted and photographed everything; then, alas, in order to see what was below, to get at the older Israelite city built immediately after the Conquest, we had to clear away all these walls, tear up the house floors and the street paving. It was rather heart-rending to see the walls of those fine houses come down, and Center Street and Dyer Street and the Fortifications disappear. We would like to keep all these walls to show every one who comes; but, in order to go on with the investigation we must reluctantly take our place among those old vandals, Shishak, Sennacherib, and Nebuchadnezzar, and destroy one of the fenced cities of Judah.

This afternoon the work of destruction began. Strict instructions were issued to watch carefully for inscribed stones which might be built into the wall, old monuments from a preceding city re-used by the Israelites to build the walls of their houses. So every workman kept a sharp lookout for *maktub*—and *bakhsheesh!* I watched the work for some time, hoping to be present when something should be found. At one time a large stone was turned over which the workmen thought *maktub,* and it did have much the appearance of a seated Egyptian statue inscribed upon it. I immediately got out the motion-picture camera to photograph this "coming out party." But the moment I show a camera every workman stands stock still. The idea of the *motion* picture has never penetrated this primitive region. The marks upon the stone proved to be wholly natural, and the picture entirely still life in a motion picture camera.

The first thing to arrest our attention was that there was but little neutral material between the debris of the city on the top and the debris of the city below. The moment we got below the floors and the streets, the distinctive pottery of Early Iron Age I began to appear. This is exactly as it ought to be, if the science of old pots in Palestine has been correctly worked out. Some would say, "Why should there be such an immediate change, as it were, in a day?" The change was not quite so sudden as in a day. When the second city succeeded the first Israelite city it would be some time, a few years perhaps, before much broken pottery would begin to accumulate in the new city. So that the change was not that of a day. It is a fact, however, that the change was in this case most clear cut. The product turned out by the potters of the kings of Judah after Shishak destroyed the first Israelite city was a definitely new product, and the old distinctive styles of Early Iron Age I passed away.

This work of destruction of an old civilization came to what threatened to be an end of civilization for the archæologist. But that is a varied story. It began with a trip to Jerusalem and three days' rest and comfort in my delightful Jerusalem home with the American Colony. There I have been entertained for the past thirty-six years, a real oasis in the desert, the same cool room year after year, the same unsurpassed table comforts, and the varied fellowship of interesting guests from all over the world. Then, also loved ones and worship and an opportunity to preach at the Sabbath service. Oh, it was joy, "glory for me."

DRIVING THROUGH A SIROCCO

Then came the journey back to camp on Monday. For the benefit of the Teacher and the *Hakim*, as well as my own benefit, not to mention throwing a little sand into the eyes of the loafers about the Jaffa gate who might note that I was returning to camp probably with money to pay the workmen, we went around by *Bab el-Wad* and Gaza on a crossroad to Beersheba's wells, and so to our destination. The first part of the journey was unalloyed pleasure; the glorious plain of Sharon and its growing crops, the rounded hills of the Shephelah, the distant mountains of Judea, the steady hum of our good engine, and the flow of pleasant and witty conversation made this first part of the day a joy.

At Gaza we were misdirected or missed the directions, I do not know which, but in any case we missed the road at Beersheba. We meandered along over camel trails until we came to the jumping-off place and had to turn back. We tried another trail which brought us to a large Bedouin camp. The Arabs proved to be friendly, offered us good water and much advice — in Arabic. However, we made out enough to know that we were not on the Beersheba road at all. Finally we persuaded a young fellow to go with us as guide. He certainly knew the way; his guttural *"Doghra, Doghra,* Forward, straight ahead," rang out like military orders. At last, there right across our path, lay the great Beersheba highway. But at the end of an hour and a half we found ourselves only seven miles from Gaza, when we ought to have been at Beersheba, thirty-eight miles away.

The road was good, the engine leaped to its task, and away we went with no traffic policeman to mark time against us. But, oh, the heat of that day. We were meeting a sirocco in the face, in the second day of its increasing fury. The temperature rose with every mile. I have experienced about 118 degrees, but that was mild weather compared with this. It must have been at least 130. We met blasts which seemed to come out of a furnace. I inadvertently touched the door of the automobile beside me and it burned my finger like a hot poker. Suddenly we topped a hill and came down to a desert pool. The water was green and greasy. Arabs floated in it, camels browsed in the swamp, and flocks sheltered beside it in "the shadow of a great rock in a weary land."

One thing helped us; the atmosphere was so dry that the great heat made almost instant the evaporation of perspiration. The skin of my hands felt actually cool to the touch, and the sun helmet with its ventilator, by the same principle of evaporation, kept the top of my head cold. Whirlwinds, little cyclones in fact, dragged their dusty tails up into the clouds. Fortunately we did not run through one of them. At last, at last, we went over a ridge and down into the oasis of Beersheba. We found a coffee-house and called for *moya, moya,* water, water. Was ever cool water more welcome; not a drop had we had since seven in the morning and it was now nearly two o'clock.

We lunched, visited *Bir Ibrahim* and two or three other wells and then turned into the Hebron-Beersheba road and in the cooler evening came on to camp *Tell Beit Mirsim*. But our troubles were not over; the sirocco had blown for two days and would continue with increasing fury one day more. That night was a night-mare. The old *Khadwadjah* slept, he always does. But there were diversions. The east wind brought a swarm of sand flies from the desert. We slept with the tent open to keep down the heat, but those little red hot wires will go through heavy bed clothes in search of me. They tattooed me like a sailor. Stinging with their bites, I waked about half way and searched in the dark for the ammonia to assuage the itching. I found a bottle and inadvertently smelled it to be sure it was ammonia. It was!

I arose early. The hot wind was blowing so that when I washed my face in water that must have been about ninety degrees, it felt as if I washed in ether, or a dash of ice-water. By wrapping a wet towel about a pitcher of water I soon had a cool drink, made so by the evaporation. Breakfast was rather a lazy affair for me. In the terrific heat and irregular meals, I had lost my appetite and was dizzy. But I struggled against the east wind up to the top of the *tell* where our workmen were doing their best to keep the work going in the awful dust. Then I climbed down the east side of the mound and retreated to the "shade of a great rock" and let the men dig away in the dust. Their persistence is most admirable; these people do not expect a soft life — and they are not disappointed. The dust cakes on my lips and my tongue cleaves to the roof of my mouth. Physically one feels like shutting up shop completely, to "crawl into a hole and pull the hole in after." But morally we cannot entertain such a disposition. It is the life one must endure, if the work is done here which needs to be done. It is all for the sake of the Book which came out of *this land*.

At 8 a. m. the mercury stood at about 100 degrees, by eleven it had mounted to 112, but an hour later it had fallen to 104. It continued to sink slowly, but was still about 100 at 4 p. m. Then with the Teacher at the wheel, I came up to Jerusalem for repairs, and to do some writing in the shade.

THE CITY THAT OTHNIEL BUILT

The contrast between the city of the kings of Judah and of that city which Othniel built after the Conquest was indeed very great. The city which Othniel rebuilt and which continued down to the time of Rehoboam to be destroyed by Shishak was an irregular, helter-skelter, squatter settlement. As it is said in the time of the Judges that every man did what was right in his own eyes, so it appears that here at Kirjath-sepher each man built his house where and how he pleased. There seems to have been no real streets, just simple paths that led around among the houses. And a large part of the space within the walls near the east gate was given up to grain pits, some of which are very large indeed. When Shishak burned the city, the greatness of the conflagration was doubtless aided by the enormous quantities of grain consumed. Does anything make a hotter or fiercer fire than burning grain? Great heaps of grain charcoal in the bottom of these pits testify to the fierceness of the fire that wrought the destruction.

The military defenses of this city were naturally more simple than of the city of the kings of Judah. Yet they were still very strong. The casemates were there, and the wall carried up for the second Israelite city seems to have been the continuation of the same wall built by Othniel. The great Canaanite wall, ten feet thick on the south side, was left by Othniel, but was not carried up on that scale.

The pottery of this period represents the best that can be said for the arts and crafts of the Israelites at this time. The types of pottery are Canaanite, especially Philistine types adopted, and perhaps in some measure adapted, by the Israelites. The beautiful ring-burnished pottery of the second Israelite city, that of the kings of Judah, was preceded in this early city by many different shapes decorated with a reddish wash. The most striking types were bowls and dishes with two handles, and the pottery with Philistine decorations, the interlocking spirals, the so-called Maltese cross, the square cross in use long before the Christian era or its late adoption by the Knights Templars, the swastika, and especially the strange swan-like bird with its neck curled around over its back. All these designs were adopted from the Philistine pottery, and the Philistines seem in turn to have adopted them from Greece and from the Cretans, at some earlier date. It thus appears clearly that the Israelites, whose arts and crafts had so greatly declined in the wilderness, learned ceramics from the Philistines. From now on for some time Philistine influence is apparent in all Israelite arts and crafts. Three periods may be discriminated: a pre-Philistine period, when little or no Philistine influence is discernible; a Philistine period, when the Philistine influence is very pronounced; and a post-Philistine period, when the Israelites became less and less dependent upon Philistine influence.

The distinguishing mark of the civilization of the Israelites at this period was certainly its markedly agricultural character. Immediately that we penetrated below the floors and street pavements of the second Israelite city there began to appear their grain pits, large and small, until a great portion of this cross-section of the *tell* was occupied by these silos. The fortress walls seem to have been used as a protected storage place for the crops rather than for any ordinary military defense. These people coming from a desert life to an agricultural land, a land "flowing with milk and honey," i. e., a land of abundance, seem first of all to have given themselves to the cultivation of the soil.

These facts of the civil life of the people in the promised land in the early days of their occupancy seem somewhat startling at first and may seem to some to give encouragement to those who have repudiated the Biblical record and have regarded the Israelites as only a few desert tribes who came into the land, and so have argued that Israel was nothing more than fragments of wandering tribes from the wilderness who had no culture whatever of any kind. A careful examination of the facts not only will not justify this theory, but it will be found that the culture discovered here is exactly in accord with the Biblical record.

That the people who came out of Egypt, according to the Exodus account, were at that time a cultured people is as clearly indicated in the narrative as it is to be expected from knowledge of the high state of such culture in Egypt at that time. It is represented that the people in the wilderness built a tabernacle. Certain persons, Bezaleel and his associates, all fellow-craftsmen and artists, were chosen because of their skill to construct the Tabernacle. The art and craft of Egypt of that period is perfectly well-known, and is hardly surpassed by that of Greece and Rome or of Medieval Europe in wood carving, in textiles, in gold or bronze work. A very brief inspection of that great collection of the works of antiquity, the Cairo Museum, is sufficient to establish this fact. That the people were agriculturists and horticulturists goes without saying of those who lived so long in Egypt. Now in the wilderness there was very little opportunity for the continuance of agricultural pursuits, though a little grain is raised in parts of the wilderness. Undoubtedly they utilized such opportunities. But for the arts and crafts, after exercising their skill in constructing the Tabernacle, their opportunities were at an end. No other tabernacle or any other building of any kind more important than a rude hut shelter here and there was constructed in the wilderness. The skilled workmen who came out of Egypt died in the wilderness. Two generations of young men grew up with no opportunity whatever to learn. Thus the arts and crafts were lost to the whole nation however large it was. But God in his providence had provided a teacher in the promised land: the Philistines, the mystery people of that ancient world, had come — from somewhere, probably from Crete — and brought the Cretan art with them. From this time on after the Conquest, the crafts of Israel bears the Philistine stamp as we have seen. They learned their arts and crafts from their neighbors.

But now new conditions confronted the people; the shepherds did not have to stray so far from home to feed their flocks; and the new and greatly enlarged opportunity for agricultural pursuits appealed to them strongly. These verdant valleys, valleys incredibly fertile, attracted them. Their enemies vanquished, they occupied the city, rebuilt the walls on a smaller scale and plunged into the appealing effort to provide themselves with grain as food for man and beast, and used this great fortress, now in their hands, as a safe place in which to store their harvests. Then they *learned* arts and crafts once more, as their clumsy efforts plainly show. Thus these rather startling conditions, indicated by the city, are only startling until the situation is clearly understood; then it is found to be exactly what the historical record demands.

In what then did consist the distinction of this people, when they entered the land? Were they really an important, not to say unique, people in any way? When God directed the great series of events called the Plagues of Egypt, which were, in fact great doings of divine providence, He did so that not only the Israelites, but the Egyptians and all the world, might know that He was the Lord.[1] When in the wilderness the Law was revealed, especially the ceremonial of the Tabernacle, it was said that the people of the land, the Promised Land, would "wonder at the great statutes." [2] Then instructions for family religion was given in the law in the words, "And these words which I command thee this day, shall be in thy heart; and thou shalt teach them diligently unto thy children, and shalt talk of them when thou sittest in thy house, and when thou walkest by the way, and when thou liest down, and when thou risest up. And thou shalt bind them for a sign upon thine hand, and they shall be as frontlets between thine eyes." [3] The whole of this history and instruction teaches, not that they were to come into the land a highly cultured people to teach the world arts and crafts and all the elements of civilization, but that they should be in their homes a God-fearing and worshiping people and that they should have for themselves and for the world a religion which for its purity and its uniqueness, should excite the wonder of the nations — The "statutes" were mainly the ceremonial law, the revelation of redemption — and that through Israel all the world might know the Lord to the end of time.

The wonders of Egypt were, indeed, the greatest exhibition of the power and authority of God as ruler of the world yet given in the history of the world and were, in fact, for all the world, a proving of God to the end of time. The "statutes," especially the ritual of the Tabernacle which is the basis of the whole ceremonial symbolical system, afterwards fulfilled in the life and work of our Lord, and unfolded in the Epistle to the Hebrews, all is in fact that wonderful message of God to a lost world at which the nations have marvelled wherever it has come. Of that home religion, we have here at Kirjath-sepher the symbols which constitute an ocular demonstration.

---

[1] *Exodus* 6:7; 7:1–5; 8:22; 9:14; 10:1–2; 14:4.
[2] *Deuteronomy* 4:5–6.
[3] *Deuteronomy* 6:6–8.

In the ruins of one of the homes of this first city of the Israelites we found that little family altar with four horns, entirely undecorated as all Israelite altars were required to be. And also a little ceremonial lamp on a tiny pedestal just high enough to serve before such family altar. The idea of a central place of worship, as the *only place where religious rites might be celebrated or an altar be placed,* receives no confirmation here.

So then, not in any preëminence in culture, but rather in the bringing in of a purer religion and a juster civil government, was the distinction of Israel at the entrance into the land. This is the distinct teaching of the Word. It nowhere countenances the idea that the Israelites were a people of unusual culture at their entrance into the land, but rather that they were a people brought in from the desert after two generations of the simple and greatly circumscribed life of "wanderers in the wilderness." It is no derogation of their importance to find the evidence of this in the ruins of Kirjath-sepher, or to state it clearly here. The idea that it was otherwise than as we have seen, is one of those extraneous ideas read into the record both by those who would unduly exalt Israel as a people, and by those who would belittle them.

If, however, the Israelites at the time of the Conquest were lacking in the gentle attainments of civilized peace, they certainly lacked nothing of the stern and furious violence of war, as is attested by the terrific destruction wrought upon the Canaanite city which was captured here by Othniel. One's curiosity is ever more and more aroused in the examination of this fortress to know, if it were possible, how long the siege of the city lasted, and some detailed account of the terrible days of the progress of the siege. That a fortress protected by such cyclopean walls, having also an adequate water supply, and, as we have seen, provided with ample facilities for storing grain, should have been easily and quickly subjugated is not to be entertained for a moment in the presence of the facts. Yet the account of the taking of the city is recited in the book of Judges in eleven words! Such is the condensation of ancient history constantly overlooked by most readers of the Bible. The sacred writers never merely gratify curiosity. We must content ourselves with the knowledge that the Egyptians once besieged nearby Sharuhen for three years.

There is no likelihood that Othniel was a victor at Kirjath-sepher in any less time.

That which we do know appallingly well is the utter ruthlessness with which the destruction of the city was wrought. Scarcely any house walls were left standing in this cross-section which we have excavated; only a few, which were re-used as house walls in the first Israelite city built here. Of these remainders of the walls, so little was left that it was with extreme difficulty that the surveyor could get sufficient bearings to discover and reconstruct with any reasonable fulness the houses and the streets of that city.

Altogether the time of the first Israelite city here down to a time some three hundred years after the Conquest, was one of great simplicity in culture, with little advancement in material things or development of military strength, and some tendency to lapse into idolatry, which was in the very blood of Israel. It was that quiet and quiescent period during which the people were trying to occupy the land and bring it under complete control, to coördinate the tribes and consolidate the government. This was a period when the great nations, Egypt on the south, the Hittites on the northwest, and Babylonia on the east, for the most part let this little land alone; and so there was no call for the development of great military strength. Most and best of all there was that quiet growth of nationalism, which became at last imperial, and of religious sentiment and home religion which burst forth with such seeming suddenness into the religious glory of the days of David and Solomon.

Last evening we returned to camp. The weather had become delightful once more, and overcoats, which a few days ago had seemed useless appendages of civilization, were in vogue again. The prospect was for a delightful night's sleep. Alas! The sand flies that had come with the storm did not go away with it. Immediately that our candle was put out, these creatures of darkness began their devilish depredations. For two hours we struggled in vain to sleep until the forehead and the back of the neck presented an appearance of smallpox with an itchiness never surpassed by that dread disease. We tried an experiment; remembering that they did not begin their attack until our light went out, we lighted our candle again and, presto, not another sting did those little pests give us. These, like other agents of malignity, could not bear the light. Most evils in this world disappear, *if we let in the light.*

GLIMPSES OF HOME LIFE

As little straws show which way the wind blows, so very little fragments of life reveal the course of civilization. Let us gather before us a small collection of the little things found at Kirjath-sepher, to see what they teach us.

These ghastly little fragments of pottery which have been through the fire of some great conflagration, from which they barely escaped with enough of themselves remaining to make known to us what they are, do not seem very attractive, yet they have a strange and far-reaching story to tell. These bits of pottery are Egyptian faience of the nineteenth dynasty, the Ramesside dynasty, during which Israel escaped at the beginning of the reign of Merenptah. How do these bits of Egyptian pottery come to be found at Kirjath-sepher? Of course, it is impossible to tell exactly how these particular bits of pottery happen to be here, but their presence here is far from surprising, and points to many interesting historical facts. It is well-known from many other places in Palestine that Egyptian influence was always in the land in that and the preceding ages. Egyptian remains are found in every excavation of ancient cities of Palestine. But this piece of faience has probably a far more interesting and intimate history than such a general observation would indicate. Israel coming from Egypt at that time to this place would quite naturally bring Egyptian relics, perhaps some of the gifts heaped upon them as they left.

We recall that Kirjath-sepher was one of the cities assigned to Caleb, and by him awarded to Othniel with his daughter, because of his heroism in taking this fenced city from the Canaanites. It is thus, as we have seen, a city inhabited at once by the incoming Israelites. And these Israelites came from Egypt of the nineteenth dynasty, to which all the Israelite events of that period belong. Whatever pottery they brought out with them was Egyptian. They themselves were Egyptians in all the arts and crafts and manners and customs of daily life. Even though they may be supposed not to have practised the arts and crafts in the wilderness life, yet not a few of the treasures brought out of Egypt would be brought into Palestine. There were hundreds of thousands of these Israelites, to put their number at the lowest possible estimate. It is, then, exactly in accord with the historical facts that we find these little fragments of decorated Egyptian pottery here. It would be surprising, almost disconcerting, if we did not find Egyptian relics among the ruins left by the Israelites of that period. Not certainly, but certainly most likely, these little fragments were once a part of the utility and the adornment of an Israelite home, a reminder of slavery days in old Egypt.

Then there is an artistic stone bowl on three feet with carved decoration. It is of beautiful shape, and seems to have been a bowl intended, or at least used, for the grinding of things with a pestle. It is like, very much like, an incense altar, but the fact that it has been ground until three holes are rubbed through, seems to stamp it unmistakably as a mortar rather than an altar. Such grinders were common then, as they are now. The mortar and pestle constitute a time-honored method of grinding foods, paints, and cosmetics. But this piece is an imitation of Egyptian work, though it is of Israelite origin. It is not to be expected that the Israelites long after the Exodus imitated Egyptian things, especially after they had developed a national consciousness and something of that exclusiveness which became at last an obsession with them. But early in their Palestinian history they may easily be thought to have imitated Egyptian things. This would be for them no more than working out in life their own imagination, which through all its ancestral training was an Egyptian imagination.

Even in the wilderness life of the Israelites, where they led almost wholly a Bedouin existence, they would still retain the art of weaving. The black and white goat's and camel's hair cloth of the Bedouin, from which all the peasants of this part of the world make the great webs out of which they construct their sprawling tents, is a common inheritance of such people. We may properly assume that the Israelites, after they came into the land and inherited "houses full of all good things," would retain and practise their knowledge of weaving.

Things have been quieter in discovery for a few days, and now there is quite a stir. It is always the unexpected that happens. In this Early Iron Age I level of the city, that which was built by the Israelites at their incoming, we have found the first oil press found anywhere here in the ruins of any age. This region is not an oil region; there are few olive trees. Apparently there never were many. It is interesting to note, however, that the Israelites on their incoming from the wilderness, where they had been so long deprived of oil, apparently made as much as possible in a small way with what few olive trees grew in the region; another glimpse of home life. The press is quite typical, following the same form and method still in vogue in this land. There is a main vat into which the oil drained from the top. Underneath this is a much smaller vat going down to a lower level, into which the sediment would settle and thus the oil be dipped off. This is exactly the settling basin principle also found in use for the clarifying of the water of their cisterns.

Strange touches of passing life are continually intruding upon us here which ought to be passed on to those who do not have the privilege of seeing for themselves. While I have been writing, a woman came up the path to a point near the entrance to our camp and stood some time looking. It may be she wished to see the *Hakim*, but she was held back by the timidity of these humble people. She had on her shoulder a baby. The little one was dirty, unkempt, infested with vermin, yet it was cuddled up in her arms as tenderly and with as much of that sweet mother love as any dainty, beruffled, dimpled darling in the cultured homes of our world.

After her came a little maid with a pitcher on her head bringing fresh goat's milk for us. She wore the white shawl over her head, as do all the *fellah* women here. Barefooted in the dust, she tripped in, straight as an Indian, and with all the grace of movement which these free-living people of the desert always display, handed the pitcher to her grandfather, who is our faithful watchman, and turned and walked away with the inimitable grace which our slouching, willowy ladies of fashion have completely lost.

Then out there in front of me is an old man, too feeble to work in the excavations, who sits in the blazing sun hour after hour, day after day, brushing and washing fragments of pottery of which he knows nothing whatever, except that his job is to make them clean, and he patiently keeps at his appointed task. He is not pretty to look at, but his faithfulness is admirable. Thus there passes before us here in this primitive life mother love in all its sweetness, grace of carriage which a princess might envy, and a faithfulness to humble duty which among us is too often conspicuous only for its absence. Of all the really noble qualities of living, these people have a goodly number, and they are the same as appear on the pages of the Book.

ISRAELITE OCCUPATION OF KIRJATH-SEPHER

Fire and sword and dust and ashes, then immediate rebuilding; such is the record of those days of the Conquest as the Bible gives it, and as we find it in the ruins.

"Thou hast given me a south land; give me also springs of water. And he gave her the upper springs, and the nether springs." Such is the record of this old city, when Othniel received it as a dower with his bride, because of his heroic assault which finally subdued this mighty fortress. This narrative involves immediate occupation of the Canaanite city by the Israelites. Othniel's bride belonged to *that generation*—the city was *her* dower. She wished to enter upon immediate possession and so, at once, her request for an adequate water supply. She was given the great wells to the north and to the south, from the latter of which we obtain water for our camp.

All of this seems simple enough in the narrative. The special interest in it arose from this, as Director Albright remarked today: "It is remarkable that it is so perfectly clear from the ruins that the Canaanite city was immediately occupied by the Israelites." Here we are digging up this old city about thirty-two hundred years after the days of the request of Caleb's daughter, which indicates immediate occupation, yet in this day, with rigid scientific tests, the thing which stands right out as a patent fact is that there was no period of decay, no long time when the place was neglected, as it has certainly been since the days of Nebuchadnezzar. There was immediate occupation; this is perceived now as we examine the ruins.

Such incidental evidences are the touchstones of a true narrative. These are the things that turn archæologists more and more toward most conservative views of the absolute

Upper: **COURTYARD OF AN "ABRAHAMIC" HOUSE WITH
DOORSOCKET *IN SITU***

Lower: **EXCAVATING AN "E" PALACE**

(Text on page 147)

PLATE XI

Upper: A BEDOUIN TENT WHERE THE STAFF WAS
ENTERTAINED

Lower: A FEAST FOR THE WORKMEN

(Text on page 157)

PLATE XII

trustworthiness of the historical narratives of the Word. Perhaps nothing will be more helpful at this point than to recite in more technical detail the evidences of immediate occupation which make it certain that there was no period of unoccupied ruins after the Israelite capture of this fortress.

I.   There is no neutral stratum between the last Canaanite city, of the Late Bronze Age and the first Israelite city, that of Othniel, in Early Iron Age I.

Accumulation of debris on the site of an unoccupied city is very rapid. It may be observed in the ruins of a burned house left to decay. It may be seen in vacant lots around the edge of any town. It is best illustrated in a land of winds and much dust. I am sitting in the shade in front of one of our tents in the early morning. The east wind is blowing, and down the street of our camp come swirls of dust every few minutes. It passes the notice of most people that such dust storms will make great accumulations and cover up things. When I go into the tent to write with my typewriter, the table must be cleared of a very cloud of dust which has accumulated in but a few minutes. This *tell* occupies the summit of a mountain. It is one of the most windy places in this land of many winds. When a sirocco blows, which it sometimes does twice a week, three days at a time and increasing in fury each day, the amount of dust accumulated on such a conspicuous spot as the top of this *tell* is amazing.

Between the first Israelite city, that destroyed by Shishak in the days of Rehoboam, and the second Israelite city which continued certainly until the days of all the various prosperous kings of Judah, there was some accumulation of neutral debris. It was not great, but there was something. It was some time after the destruction by the Egyptian Shishak, before Rehoboam or his successor rebuilt the city.

Here, when we cleared away the rubbish of the first Israelite city down to the bottom, it was to be expected, ordinarily, that there would be a neutral layer of rubbish, that is, rubbish having in it no remains of human occupation, simply the dust of ages. *There was absolutely none.* Immediately below the ruins of the first Israelite city appeared the ruins of the last Canaanite city. So there had been no period of an unoccupied city here.

II. The new city of Othniel rests immediately upon the *ashes* of the city destroyed. The most terrible burning revealed by this city in all its history is that which occurred when Othniel took the city. The history of that siege and final assault has never been written, except as it is written here in the ashes and charcoal and lime. It is most pathetic, appalling indeed, to contemplate the awful destruction which must have taken pace, raged here, at the final assault on the city. Here we have direful marks of the demon fire: a deep layer of ashes and charcoal from the timbers of the doors and roofs of the houses, fragments of brick from the upper stories, and great heaps of lime from the action of fire upon the limestone of which the walls were built. This shows what burning would do. As far as we have cleared the city inside the east gate down to this level, about two thousand square meters, a layer of ashes continues over the whole surface of all that portion inside the east gate, the chariot entrance to the city.

Now this layer of ashes is immediately under the ruins of the first Israelite city. It is well known that in the whole early history of Palestine, the ground was never cleared for the rebuilding of the city. The new constructions were laid immediately upon whatever was in sight whether on the ruins of the just destroyed city, or on an accumulation from ages of windstorms. So these houses of Othniel's city were built immediately upon this layer of ashes and all the gruesome collection of remains. The new city rose literally out of the ashes of the old. Here again we have conclusive evidence of the immediate occupation of the city after it was conquered by Othniel. The daughter of Caleb asked *at once* that she be given "springs of water." "So he gave her the upper springs and the nether springs."

III. Some of the Late Bronze walls are re-used and carried right up into the houses.

When the Israelites came in under Othniel and prepared to occupy the city, they made use of what was to their hand. Some of the old Canaanite walls protruded above the ashes of the burned city. These the Israelites seized upon for their own use. They were not themselves good builders. Those generations born in the wilderness had not built houses. Naturally enough they took advantage of every standing wall.

So that, in fact, some of the houses which they erected were simply Canaanite constructions carried up to a higher level.

This is shown in a curious manner which reveals much of the way in which they lived and the conditions round about them. The Israelites used the city, as we have seen, after their occupation of it largely as a place for storing the grain of the surrounding agricultural region. They made many grain pits. The dwelling houses were a helter-skelter lot of houses of squatters, without any city planning whatever. Each man built his house to suit his own convenience or thoughtless fancy. They made no regular streets at all, but moved about among the houses as people move about in a crowd. They did, in the end, learn the ways of civilized life in settled houses and cities, but at the beginning their desert habits were dominant. So they made many pits for the storing of grain as they had probably sometimes done for the little garden patches of grain which they had been able to raise in the desert life. So there were made these many grain pits. Sometimes they dug them down deep into the ruined cities that lay below them. The pottery and other rubbish thrown out in such excavations were left to mingle with their own pottery, and is found there now in the ruins. Thus in the ruins of the Israelite city there are found a good many pieces of pottery of the Canaanite cities preceding. But in these grain pits, used only by the Israelites who dug them, there is *absolutely no pottery, but their own.* Now, by comparison of this Israelite pottery from the grain pits with the Canaanite pottery thrown out at the time the grain pits were dug, it is possible to determine exactly *where the Canaanite level ceased and the Israelite occupation began,* and thus to trace the Canaanite walls which are carried up above this level, and to see also that the line of division between Canaanite and Israelite levels is exactly on the ashes, and hence that there was immediate occupation.

RECONSTRUCTION OF KIRJATH-SEPHER

Scientific people are rather inclined to shy off from reconstructions, as involving too much imagination, but without such reconstruction it is difficult for the non-technical reader to acquire a realizing conception of such a fortress as Kirjath-sepher, when it stood in its might. Besides, the reconstruction to be presented is a strictly scientific reproduction. An artist was brought from Jerusalem who was instructed in the width of the ruin and the character of the fortifications and was shown Egyptian pictures of Palestinian fortifications. He then took photographs and made drawings to measurement and from all this material made a crayon drawing which was then photographed and is here reproduced.

The fortress presents a truly formidable aspect and is certainly very accurate in its representations, even to the bastions and towers which are copied from Egyptian sculptures. At sight of such a stronghold we note the significance of the laconic statement of the Biblical writer, that "the whole army" came here to take Kirjath-sepher. The Bible represents that to have been a great army, and surely no little band of Bedouin raiders from the desert tribes would ever be able to take this fortress. Moreover, the "whole army" must have required from three to five years to subdue this place, wearing down the garrison by hand to hand fighting and starving them out by long investment. Thus does such a reconstruction give the last touch of realism to the brief Biblical narrative of the taking of Kirjath-sepher and the completion of the Conquest.[4]

---

[4] ALBRIGHT, *Annual of American Schools of Oriental Research*, Vol. XII, pp. 52, 56.

CHAPTER V

THE LAST OF THE CANAANITES

SCARABS AND CULT OBJECTS, LEVEL "C"

Camp Tell Beit Mirsim.

I HAVE said that when we came here this year for excavations, we retired into the Patriarchal Age. To many, that doubtless seemed an exaggerated metaphor. It will help much to understand the Patriarchal city we are now uncovering (for yesterday we began to dig out the city that Othniel took), if we get a vivid picture of the actual Patriarchal life going on around about us in ordinary affairs. The vestibule of the ancient land of the Book is the present-day land of the Book. Archæology might be defined as the science of old, dead things, except for one thing: that many of the old things *are not yet dead.* We would miss much of the ancient life of this land, if we only observed what comes out of the pit we are digging and the dust we are groping in. A vast deal of the ancient life still lives about us and this, also, we must add to the record of the excavations, else the picture will not be complete.

Harvest was drawing near, the grain was whitening, here and there beginning to turn golden for the sickle. Some of the fields of wheat were most cheering to the farmer; the grain stood three to four feet in height and the heads were bursting with the plumpness of the kernels of wheat. Other fields were not so promising and, having been planted later, the heads were not yet filled out. Still, the farmer lived in hope. The farmer is a man of hope. There are too many elements in the problem of his life, which are not calculable, for him to be quite sure about anything. It would be well for all of us, if we realized this more in all things. The desire to be insured against all sorts of contingencies has become a kind of obsession and people hardly perceive it. After all, it is the desire to escape responsibility, to do just what the race has been trying to do ever since that first dreadful day of sin in the world, *pass the responsibility to some one else.*

So these farmers lived in hope, until one dreadful day and night; that day when we came from Gaza to Beersheba in 130 degrees of heat, and the night that followed, when the wind tossed our camp and threatened to demolish it, and the sand flies bit me until I have looked like a smallpox victim ever since. It was the sirocco, the dreaded hot east wind, the destroying blast from the *Kedem.* In that one day and night the farmer learned what the harvest would be. Every stalk of grain was dried in the field. That which was already filled out and beginning to ripen was immediately ripened; that which was still green was completely cured without ripening; made dry as tinder, still retaining, in large measure, its green color. Such is the "east wind" given such a terrible character by the prophets and historians of Bible lands.

Harvest began at once. The number of our workmen diminished, for the men must save their crops. Life is reduced to its simplest elemental problems here. In America, and many other parts of the world, the problem of life is how, in a thousand ways, to make money. The problem here is to produce food, to fetch water, to buy clothing, and to make shelter. Now the immediate task was to produce food for man and beast. And so the harvest began at once.

The reaper went forth to the broad fields. But it was not a McCormick or a Deering — it was a sickle, just like the sickles that came out of the great cistern in the plaza of the second Israelite city up on the *tell,* thrown there perhaps in the vain hope, that, after the enemy had done his worst, they might be recovered. Just such sickles the farmers and their wives and their sons and daughters are wielding all around us here.

No raker is needed after the reapers. They are all "self-rakers"; for they gather the grain into little sheaves as they cut it and then twist a few straws around the sheaf to hold it together. Then they drop the sheaves, when they are finished, and later gather them into great heaps. Then comes a great camel, nine or ten feet high, meandering along with his soft, cat-like tread and measured pace as though he had all eternity in which to do his task. Indeed, he always takes his task just that way, except when he becomes frightened, and then he runs as if all the demon world was at his heels, as frantic as any runaway horse.

He is indeed a great camel, but ofttimes he is driven — perhaps engineered would be a more appropriate word — by a tiny maiden who does not come up to his knees. Here is a most striking illustration of man's dominion over the beasts. She taps him on the right side or on the left and he turns accordingly, or she whacks his legs with her stick as high as she can reach, if he is unmindful of her hints. At her soft breathing "hh, hh," he folds up his ungainly legs and sits down to wait patiently for his load. A net is spread over his saddle and down his sides and then the great heap of sheaves is loaded upon him until sometimes only close inspection can discover the camel. But he is enjoying himself; the old inhibition not to muzzle the ox that treadeth out the corn is sedulously observed in this land. And the camel seems to know it, for he turns his supercilious lips around to the heap on his back and takes a mouthful of the grain as often as he wishes and is not even chided for it. When the load on his back is half as big as an American farmer builds on his hay ladders, the net is roped tightly around all. Another softly breathed hint is given the camel and suddenly that great heap of sheaves rustles and sways like a house in an earthquake and, lo, the camel's long neck and legs and tail appear and the whole heap moves off toward the threshing floor. Just such a harvest field as this was that which Joseph saw in his dream;[1] such also as lay before Samson, when he set fire to the dry fields of ripening grain of the Philistines.[2]

I was by my tent one day when my attention was drawn to a poor woman on the slope of the revetment wall of the *tell*. A little grain is raised on some parts of the *tell*, and the camels had come down the revetment slope with their burdens of sheaves on the way to the threshing floor beyond our camp. Now and again a straw with a head of wheat or barley dropped by the wayside, and this poor woman was patiently picking them up one by one and putting them in the bosom of her gown, or making the straws into a little sheaf. She was a gleaner, as was Ruth in the fields of Boaz. A member of our staff visited a poor little store in the cave

---

[1] *Genesis* 37:5–8.
[2] *Judges* 15:3–5.

village near by. There came in a little maiden who emptied from the sleeve of her gown a few handfuls of grain which the storekeeper took and added to his bin and gave her in return a handful of candy! Half piasters are far too valuable to give to children for sweetmeats, but the children *will get them somehow*. This little one had probably gleaned these handfuls of grain to gratify her longing for the sweets of life.

An old man among our neighbors motioned to me one day to come to the threshing-floor. I suspected that he had something which he wished me to photograph, but I was little prepared for the scene that he laughingly showed me. The men had two young cows lying on their backs, had tied all four feet of each cow together, and were proceeding to shoe the cows to tread out the grain as described in Micah: "I will make thy hoofs brass." [3] Little pieces of metal were fastened on the divided hoofs by great hobnails. Then these two cows and a donkey were driven together round and round until the grain was trodden out.

Now they must wait for the wind. How absolutely the farmer must work with Providence. When the wind blows well, they toss the heap of straw and chaff into the air again and again and again until the heap has become two heaps, one of straw and chaff and the other of grain and finer chaff. Then a man, sometimes a woman, patiently sifts the heap of grain from the chaff still mixed with it, loads the donkey or camel with the great sacks of grain, and goes away home, exactly as Joseph's brethren fetched grain from Egypt.[4] Some people try to argue from the great freight trains of Europe and America that grain could not thus be brought from Egypt. But in this land there was, and ordinarily still is, *no other way*. Thus they now bring up watermelons on camels. They succeeded then as they succeed now. These people do not eat as much as we do. I think we members of the staff eat as much as twenty of the workmen. Yet these men are strong. They live in the open. They have few diseases and do not have to combat with food and stimulants the poisons of indoor life. Most of the disease germs are hothouse bred; they do not grow in the wild.

Yet with all the poverty of these people and the hardship

---

[3] *Micah* 4:13.
[4] *Genesis* 42–45.

in which they live, they invite us to feast after feast, and feed us bountifully.

Interesting are these additional fragments of iron sickles, some with the rivets still present which fastened the blade to the wooden handle, and in one instance a sliver of the wood still clings. Around about us are scores of men and women and boys and girls using just such sickles with which to cut their poor sirocco-burned harvest. And these plowshares, broken, indeed, but complete in fragments, have also traces of wood upon which the share was fitted. When we came here in April the farmers were still plowing for dura, the great summer crop of corn; they were using plows with just such shares as these.

Now we have gotten below the ashes down to the Canaanite level in the ruins of the ancient city. The gruesome marks of the burning by Othniel are most suggestive of the terrible conflict that raged here for months, perhaps for years, before this old fortress fell into the hands of the Israelites. So completely did they destroy the Canaanite city in this part near the gate that at first it was well-nigh impossible to get any idea of the character of the city at all. Not until William the Scribe, the surveyor, puts his compass and his level upon these walls, will we be able clearly to discover the plan of the houses. Little by little, however, it soon appeared that the Israelites, finding some Canaanite walls protruding above the debris, did utilize them and carried them up as the walls of their own houses. These re-used walls displayed much better building than that done by the Israelites themselves. Immediately below this Israelite city and the layer of ashes, Bronze Age pottery at once begins to appear.

KIRJATH-SEPHER OF THE RULE OF THE PHARAOHS

Yesterday was Egyptian day at the *tell*. In fact, as we have now gotten down to the Late Bronze Age, when Palestine was an Egyptian province, immediately we find Egyptian influence everywhere apparent. It is not that we find so many things that are really Egyptian in origin, but the sculptors and artists manifest the Egyptian motif. Egyptian things were imitated in Palestine, and sometimes purely Egyptian things are found.

That tell-tale layer of ashes reported in the account of the stratification of the mound now displays all its historical significance. It is, indeed, one of the most decisive pieces of archæological evidence of the history of culture which the whole progress of discovery has disclosed. Most pieces of evidence reveal each one thing only; this tells us indeed many things. It is a veritable revelation in dust and ashes. This great layer of ashes indicates a great burning. Was it only a conflagration or was it a conquest? The debris below and above this level indicates totally different civilizations. Here is an absolute and total and immediate change of culture; hence this conflagration indicates a conquest which introduced a new civilization. Everything below this level is Canaanite, all the pottery, all the implements, all the weapons. Above the ashes everything is Israelite, all the pottery, all the implements, all the weapons. Hence the Conquest was an Israelite conquest of Canaanite civilization. Moreover, as this culture is continued onward to "A" level of the time of the kings of Judah, and as there was no neutral layer of debris above the ashes, and hence there was immediate occupation after the burning that produced these ashes, this conquest must have been *the* Conquest at the incoming of the Israelites, when Othniel commanded under Joshua. Last of all, and perhaps most important of all, no iron was in the debris below this layer of ashes; bronze was absolutely universal for weapons and implements. Above this layer of ashes, the bronze gives way for most such purposes to iron. Only for jewelry was bronze used. Manifestly this Conquest in the days of Joshua was just at the incoming of the Iron Age. This is exactly in accord with the representation of the Biblical records that the Israelites had to contend with the iron chariots of the Canaanites.[5]   That the Philistines held a monopoly of the iron business is shown by the hard conditions they imposed upon the Israelites, in that no smithy was permitted in Israel far along in the time of the Judges.[6]

This certainly fixes the Conquest at this place, Kirjath-sepher, at the beginning of the Iron Age. This does not absolutely fix the time of the Conquest throughout the land — for we do not know exactly how long a time was consumed in the conquest of the land under Joshua — and thus the

[5] *Joshua* 17:16, 18.
[6] *I Samuel* 13:19–21.

time of the Exodus forty years earlier. *Until, however, undoubted Israelite remains be found in connection with Bronze Age material, we will have to hold to the Iron Age for the whole work done under Joshua.*

So yesterday at one point in the excavations as the workmen were digging down into the Late Bronze, level "C," immediately a very important cult object appeared, something that apparently belonged to a temple, or at least to a Canaanite altar. It is in the form of a plaque that is in reality a small offering table not intended for meat or meal offering, but for the pouring of libations. It is a grotesque object, as an art work having but very little merit, but as a cult object, showing the Canaanite religion of the time, it is very important. It is ornamented by a lioness and two cubs. They are grotesque, rather comical, indeed, in their artistic character They plainly follow the Egyptian idea of ornamenting sacrificial tables with lions, but an Egyptian artist would have been disgusted with the Palestinian form of his art. The lioness has a sardonic grin which looks like a cross between the snarl of a cat and the smirk of a frog, and the cubs are given human forearms and hands in the place of forelegs. The worship at this altar may have been very solemn in character, but it seems to me that the priests must have laughed every time they looked at that comical lioness.

In the same Late Bronze level and representing the same period in history, there was found a very beautiful real Egyptian scarab. It is a work of art exquisitely well-done, a royal scarab, indeed. Moreover, it was not a chance ornament, but was a seal scarab. The fastenings by which it was joined to the seal ring still remain. It was thus the property of an Egyptian official in Palestine, whom we would call, I suppose, a consul or vice-consul at Kirjath-sepher. The royal cartouche is that of Amenophis III. In addition to the cartouche name and the title, "lord of two lands," he is given a special title, "rising over all foreign countries," the royal title on the seal of the representatives of the government in a foreign province.

This little Egyptian object, with its royal cartouche and title, is most significant historically. It shows very clearly that at that time Palestine was still an Egyptian province. **The Israelites** had not yet occupied the land, nor had that other falling away from Egypt taken place which occurred in the reign of Amenophis IV, the heretic king Akhnaton, which is also reflected in the *Tell el-Amarna* tablets. The date of the reign of Amenophis III is well established as a little before, and a little after, the beginning of the fourteenth century. This parallels very accurately the Biblical history. The scarab's exact date, however, cannot be determined from this or, as yet, from any other evidence. This scarab indicates a date after the accession of Amenophis III, and as it was an official seal scarab *most probably* indicates that he was still on the throne. But scarabs, even royal scarabs, were sometimes made at a later date, even after the death of the king whose name they bear.

We should note that this official scarab might have an important bearing on the never-ending discussion about the time of the Exodus and the Conquest. It is, however, not conclusive, although students who hold that the Exodus took place in the reign of Amenophis III, in fact near the beginning of his reign, will find considerable difficulty in accommodating the idea that the Israel tablet of Merenptah represents Israel at that time to be in Palestine (as they interpret Merenptah's tablet) to the significance of this scarab which so plainly indicates that, during the reign of Amenophis III or soon after, Palestine was still in Egyptian hands and that an Egyptian consul was at a peasant town in Palestine.

Occasionally we find scarabs and scaraboids that are Palestinian imitations of Egyptian ones, showing, of course, Egyptian influence, but themselves very inartistic. Quite occasionally we find real Egyptian scarabs, like the Amenophis scarab and this little symbolical scarab of the New Empire. It is a serpent scarab of the eighteenth dynasty, and comes from the city destroyed by Othniel, the last city of the Canaanites, "C" level. It is another link in the chain of evidence that this city was still under the control of the Egyptian government until the end of the Late Bronze Age, and that the Israelites did not come in during that Age at all.

Kirjath-sepher never was an artistic center. It was merely a peasant town. Nevertheless, occasionally we find objects of considerable refinement and culture, evidence of people who loved and possessed pretty things. These tiny fragments of gold leaf which the sharp eyes of the workmen have fished out of the dust and rubbish, were used in some way by some persons for some beautiful things. They did not put gold leaf on pots and pans. This brings to mind a thought which stirred me the other day: What are the necessaries of life and what are the luxuries? In this land a siesta, a little quiet sleeping time in the middle of the day, is not one of the luxuries, but one of the necessities of life. The members of the staff take a siesta in the tents, and the workmen on the mound have an hour after their lunch for a siesta. But just here the line of demarcation between necessaries and luxuries is betrayed. We like a cot or a reclining chair or at least a seat in a breezy place in the shade; but here before me is our *Haj,* our watchman, lying in the shade of our reed workshop on the bare ground in the dust with a stone for a pillow and he seems to be sleeping like a babe in its cradle; and —amazing!—our workmen up on the mound are for the most part sitting or lying out in the open sun on the dust of the excavated debris where the temperature is 125 in the sun, and they are asleep, too! What is luxury? All the refinements of life are comparative.

Many duties come to us by the wayside. The men are often hurt at their work. Occasionally somebody is bitten by a scorpion. And so with a small supply of medicine our *Hakim,* or some one of the staff who plays *Hakim,* endeavors to heal the hurts of the people around. This fact is reported among the people of the community, and little ones with mashed fingers and stubbed toes are brought by their loving fathers to the *Hakim;* patient, stoical little creatures they are. Sometimes this work becomes burdensome; but we cannot help feeling that we should give a somewhat wide interpretation to our Lord's words, "Suffer the little children, and forbid them not, to come unto me." So we try to heal their hurts and ills.

A Spectacular Find

On a later occasion, description of the excavation had been completed, I was back once more in Jerusalem, and the staff were all preparing to break camp, filling in, loading the antiquities and camp paraphernalia, when one of our Egyptian foremen made a last-minute find, the spectacular discovery of "C" level and the Late Bronze Age. A **few feet** from the place where was found the offering table with the lion decoration, an image of a lioness sculptured in fine limestone appeared. It is a crouching lioness, uninscribed. Lions are frequently mentioned in the Bible, and formed the supports to the throne chair of Solomon, and the lioness is often figured as a goddess of Canaan or of Egypt in Egyptian sculpture. It is impossible as yet certainly to determine the significance of this, the first lion of this age found in Palestine. There is a strong presumption that it is an idol, a lion goddess; it was found near the offering table which certainly was used before an idol; and the decoration of the offering table had a lion motif, and so it would be appropriate to be used to serve a lioness goddess. This spectacular find, when added to the exceedingly informing history of culture that this season has yielded, makes a gratifying appeal to the public, which dearly loves to *see things*.

Again there is an accumulation of a multitude of little things, little in the physical sense, but sometimes great, and always cumulative, in the information they give us concerning the life of the people. Arrow heads may reveal to us something of the dangers of the times, and hairpins, and needles, and gold leaf, trifles though they are, are very suggestive of some degree of refinement and culture. This tiny idol, probably a pendant or a pocket piece, nevertheless an idol, coming from the Canaanite period immediately preceding the incoming of the Israelites, is very suggestive concerning the low level to which their idolatrous practices had descended. However repulsive the worshipping of images at any time may be to our susceptibilities, it is quite possible to realize that simple-minded, unlettered people might be frightened into a worshipful attitude by a great and hideous idol; but how any sane human being could come into a frame of mind that could worship a god that he carried around in his pocket is rather incomprehensible. The lowest, most ignorant tribes on earth today have not descended below that level.

CHAPTER VI

THE AGE OF TURMOIL

Hyksos Mysteries, Level "D"

Camp *Tell Beit Mirsim.*

SOME folks think of the field work of an archæologist as, indeed, veritable dry-as-dust, serious, scientific work and dull study, enough to give one a daily headache and nights of terrible nightmares. Other folks think the archæologist one most enviable person from the privileged classes of the world, one who gets delightful journeys up and down this old world and is feasted and feted like a king. These are the deluded folk who write me every year before I come abroad and declare themselves possessed of an insatiable desire to come along, a desire that just must be gratified and will not be denied, for — "they want to see things!" Still others imagine that the life of the archæologist must be an intolerable hardship, unconscionable boredom, poking about in old caves full of fleas, digging up old ruins and robbing graves full of mouldy skulls with teeth dropping out, — ugh! Others think the life all tragedy, and still others, all comedy; and the rest, indeed, most folks, think it as uninteresting as a hopelessly dull lecture on fans.

Now, in fact, the life of the archæologist is none of these things, and yet all of these things and much more. I am going to tell you about it. There will be nothing archæological, or technical, or scientific about some of this account; it is to be in the lightest vein. And yet, it is *part of the Story of the culture of Bible Lands into which Bible narratives must fit.*

Episodes are numerous at camp in the wild. Something startling is due at almost any moment. They come humorous, pathetic, and tragic. This one was near-tragic with a humorous ending. Yesterday I saw a woman winnowing grain by lifting it with her hands and letting it fall, the wind carrying away much of the dust and chaff. A little child and a kid played by her. It made a pretty picture and I took my moving picture camera to get a photograph. While my eye was on the finder and my ear open to the hum of the motor, suddenly the woman ran away, and the baby and kid scurried, too. I looked up to see where they had gone, and was startled to see a very determined looking man followed by several others rushing toward me with big stones in their hands which they were already throwing. I thought they were offended at my photographing the woman, and concluded that I was in serious trouble. But they were trying to stone some venomous reptile, snake or viper, from which the woman and child had fled. The men searched most diligently and carefully for that reptile, but did not find it. That was once I was glad for a snake!

A new week, like a new year, gives a new starting-point. The Sabbath of rest, a rapidly increasing number of workmen, from fifty to sixty, to eighty, and then to one hundred, and the ground cleared of debris, all worked together to start off another week with zest.

The period in the ruins before the Late Bronze Age, the time of the Judges, and the Monarchy, back through the Middle Bronze Age, the time of the Patriarchs, has been one of great perplexity. There seems to have been a troubled time with much turmoil and destruction and re-building, but no distinct change of culture. Through a complex system of strata, everything was Middle Bronze. The patriarchs were moving about the land; then Israel was in Egypt, the Hyksos kings were on the throne in Egypt and probably also a dominant influence here; yet no foreign culture supplanted the native. All this points to civil strife. Doubtless there were politicians with ambitions then as now, uprisings, coups d'etat and revolutions then as in all other ages and lands. We seem to have come upon the remains of "Middle Ages" in the civilization of Palestine, comparable on a very much smaller scale to the breaking up of the Roman Empire, the Feudal Period, and the re-alignment that followed and is still following.

At least we came in the excavation of this part of the *tell* to a great burned level, a distinct and more extended memorial of fire. When we go below that tell-tale layer of ashes and charcoal we shall find something different; perhaps the Early

Upper: **THE STAFF, 1932**
Left to right, Gad, Gordon, Detweiler, Bright, Stinespring,
Liggitt, Broyles, Schmidt
Seated, Kelso, Albright, Kyle, Glueck
Lower: CAMP *TELL BEIT MIRSIM,* 1932

(Text on page 165)

PLATE XIII

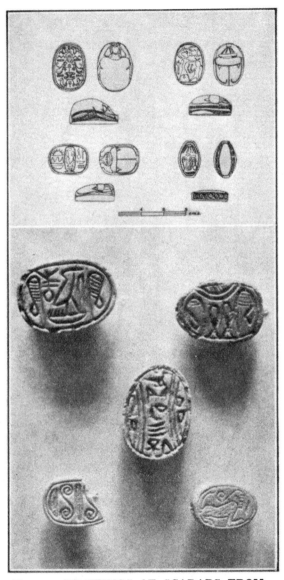

Upper: **DRAWINGS OF SCARABS FROM "C" AND "D" LEVELS**

Lower: **PHOTOGRAPHS OF SCARABS FROM "E" LEVEL. "JACOB" SCARAB IN CENTER**

(Text on page 175)

PLATE XIV

Bronze Age remains, toward which we are certainly approaching.

A burned level — always we go forward in this work by burned levels. Always history progresses by "burned levels." Oh, it ought not to be so; it is a rebuke to human perversity that it is so, an incontestable evidence of a quarrelsome race of sinners. Why else should progress be by strife, and not by coöperation? Nietzsche's philosophy of history we must utterly repudiate; but the fact remains to confront a guilty world at the judgment day that progress as well as decline in civilization is marked by "burned levels." The imperial splendor of Khammurabi, of Rameses, of Sennacherib, of Alexander, of Cæsar was followed by the burning. Greek art and architecture and literature all were followed by a great darkness, a "burned level." So in Roman history, as, indeed, in the glory that was Solomon's, and among the Pharaohs.

TURMOIL OF THE HYKSOS PERIOD

The appalling strife and turmoil of the Middle Bronze Age, the time of the Patriarchs, and the happy sojourn of Israel in Egypt as the guests of the kings, monarchs of the Hyksos Dynasty — for a long time these things have been suspected, then began to be manifest, but never before have they been so completely and tragically displayed as in the ruins of this old city. In that Middle Bronze Age we found one city, then two, then three, and now four, and we are wondering if, when we go below this last level, we may find even another within a period of about three hundred years. The poverty of the cities is sometimes evidenced by the substitution of brick for stone in the walls, and by the irregularity of the walls. Here is hoping that we may yet find, not only evidence of the troubled times of the Hyksos, but a positive determination of the ethnic character of those mysterious people, whence they came, and how great was their dominion, and exactly what the relationship of the Israelites was with them. In the meantime we may well keep in mind an item from the first of these letters, namely the similarity of Philistine pottery to Cypriote pottery, of Cypriote to Hittite, and of Hittite pottery to Greek pottery of the region of Troy. If we can find out from which one of these the others copied or whether they all copied from another, and who that other was, then we shall know who these Hyksos were and whence they came, for the pottery was this beautiful Middle Bronze pottery of the Hyksos times found everywhere with them.

The present is frankly a time of puzzlement in our work. Perhaps some would say nothing about it until all is cleared up. But I have undertaken to keep the readers of these letters with me in all the perplexities day by day. Why, then, should they not see this puzzlement and have the pleasure of trying to solve the puzzle and the joy of saying, "That is just what I thought," when the difficulty is resolved.

Manifestly there were wars, wars, wars. So it seems as we look back over the three hundred years covered by Middle Bronze. It will not seem so warlike an age, if we remember that we in America think ourselves a very peaceful people, and yet our wars have not been *fifty years apart*. The greater puzzlement, however, is that, although the distinctive Middle Bronze pottery is unmistakable all through these many cities, yet Early Bronze types have been appearing increasingly as we go back toward the Early Bronze Age. Ordinarily the different ages are quite distinct in the layers of debris, and have been especially so here at Kirjath-sepher. When we went below the Early Iron II to Early Iron I, the time of the Judges, the culture changed abruptly, there was hardly any mixing of types. So, when we went on down to the Late Bronze, it was with only a little mixing of types, and on to Middle Bronze with the same experience. But between Middle Bronze and Early Bronze it is different, startlingly different; four layers already in Middle Bronze and an increasing mixture of types as we draw near the next layer below.

We found the same phenomenon at *Bab ed-Dra*[1] and at the Moabite temple at Ader, that is, in the civilization of the cities of the Plain and in subsequent civilization in Moab. On the Plain it was wholly Early Bronze, in Moab there was a mixture as here, Early Bronze types among Middle Bronze types. Are these Early Bronze types hold-over pieces which continued in Middle Bronze for a time? Or did Middle Bronze not come in suddenly with a great catastrophe, but gradually, only in a long time wholly displacing the Early Bronze types? If the latter is the solution, it would seem to be in accord with

---

[1] KYLE, *Explorations at Sodom*, Chapter V.

the age of turmoil during the domination of the Hyksos in Egypt and throughout this Near East. If they brought in the Middle Bronze types, then the civilization during all the age of turmoil was struggling against them and only in three hundred years succumbed. We will think of these things and, when we dig on down, as we shall do within a few days, we shall probably know the answer, and may also know more about the Hyksos.

Before I could get this written there was brought in from some of the diggers, who were working on an isolated section of the "A" level on the *tell,* another of those interesting historical, inscribed jar handles, "To Eliakim, the official servant of Jehoiachin," who only reigned three months and eight days. The first of these was found here early in 1928. A second was found by Dr. Grant at Beth Shemesh; and here is now the third. It begins to appear that Jehoiachin, who was king so short a time and is given such scant notice, was at the head of a very effective administration in force in widely separated parts of his kingdom. These are the most valuable of discoveries, for while inscriptions may have false statements in them, as men will lie, events never conspire together for any purpose; they always give the facts.

And now the great truth of the history of this land, its civilization and its culture as well as its Biblical history, begins to be ever more and more apparent; the Hyksos age was the age of turmoil in all this wide portion of Bible lands, from the valley of the Nile to the dual land of the Euphrates and the Tigris. The Hyksos were favorable to the sons of Jacob, and seemingly, like Ishmael, in all the rest of the world of their time, their hand was against every man's hand. The Egyptians hated them and struggled against their domination; and the oppression of Israel, when the Hyksos were driven out, was no doubt in some measure an aftermath of hate now that the royal patrons of the Israelites were gone. But the tragic domination of the Hyksos was by no means confined to Egypt; Palestine and Syria and possibly far-away lands of the Euphrates valley were made to feel their power and, if disposed to resist, also their ruthlessness. The Bible speaks of them only in Egypt and does not give them any ethnic name even there. But the spade is writing much history around about the Biblical story to illuminate it. Here at Kirjath-

sepher, in the debris of the Middle Bronze Age, while the
Israelites were in Egypt as favorites of the Hyksos kings, the
Hyksos pottery and scarabs clearly indicate their influence.
Here was long drawn out strife though the culture did not
change. There had evidently been civil strife, most probably
uprisings against the oppressor, which were ruthlessly suppressed with siege and burning. These tell-tale burned layers
are tragic in suggestion. It becomes ever-increasingly evident
that the Hyksos were the Scythians of the ancient world, ruthless hordes from somewhere in the north which swarmed
over the lands, as the Huns over central Europe in medieval
times.

And now comes the deduction from this induction of facts.
At *Bab ed-Dra* in 1924 we had found the Great High Place
of the Cities of the Plain, and there secured a large collection
of potsherds which were identified as Early Bronze and the
beginning of Middle Bronze. This in a definite way, but with
a considerable margin of time, certified the Abrahamic history and the destruction of the Cities of the Plain. Here now,
at Kirjath-sepher, we have identically the same types of pottery, and mingled with them the well-known Hyksos types,
and this in the beginning of the Middle Bronze Age and the
end of the Early Bronze, here also positively dated. This
confirms exactly our conclusions concerning the destruction
of the Cities of the Plain. Let us hope that we may also,
before the end of this campaign, get something, like the
burning made by Othniel, that will date the destruction of
the cities as exactly as that which dated the Conquest at the
very beginning of the Iron Age in Palestine.

THE SERPENT GODDESS

A quiet Sabbath service was in progress in "a large upper
room" in Jerusalem. It was my privilege to conduct that
service. It was a memorable occasion, not for the sermon,
though I love to preach, but for the news which broke into
the serenity of that service at the close. The news was
brought in by him whom our workmen insist on calling "the
Jew," Dr. Schmidt, the Danish gentleman. He was excited
almost to the point of incoherent ecstasy. His blundering
English and almost inarticulate pronunciation, with a strange
mixture of Danish and German words, made it impossible to

understand more than half of what he said. There was something about "temple" and "snake" and "tree." Only one thing was perfectly clear, and that was that a great discovery, something really startling and important, has been made at the camp.

Monday morning early saw us on the great Hebron-Beersheba road and the long camel trail that leads up from the road to the camp, that we should discover what this great thing might be. Director Albright met us with an exultant smile and enthusiasm of the "lighter-than-air" variety. It seemed almost a wonder that he could keep his feet on the ground. At once he called us into the dining-tent and lifted the find from its carefully guarded resting-place, as proudly as a father with his first baby. It was a cult object of Canaanite worship, a white limestone stele about a foot wide and of an original height that cannot yet be known, as the top is broken away. The stele is sculptured in beautiful low relief which, because of the wearing effect of the lime in the debris, makes it rather difficult to see clearly what is on it. Even a glance, however, was enough to show it to be an entirely unique and remarkable monument of pure Canaanite cult. There is no trace of any Egyptian or other influence, as usually is found in cult objects of Palestine. When I informed Professor Fisher of our find his exclamation was spontaneous, "Oh, you have the serpent, have you?" Here for the first time a distinct feature of purely Canaanite worship, without any admixture of foreign ideas, has been found. There is what at first seemed a large tree-trunk, the top of which is broken off, but which, when the lime was brushed off, proved to be a god or goddess, and around which a great serpent is coiled. An artist's crayon drawing brought out distinctly the appearance of the sculpture. The result was little less than marvelous. The horrid loathsomeness of Canaanite worship stood revealed before us. The hope of finding the remainder of the monument, on which was the head of this horrid divinity, is very remote. The stone is limestone, and the part we have shows severe marks of fire. Probably the remainder was turned into lime, of which we find bushels in the ruins. Although we cannot at this time excavate the house in which the monument was found, it was perhaps a temple. Only there would such a monument probably be found.

At last we had something unusual, something of unique importance in Palestinian archæology. If we had found nothing else in the two seasons of our work here (and we have in fact hundreds of other objects, many of much importance) this alone would have sufficed for all our work and our outlay. We had longed and prayed for some really great discovery, now we certainly had it. We could hardly sleep, which is saying a great deal for the old *Khawadjah*.

The elements of the importance of this cult object do not lie on the surface, and its significance will not appear to those who are simply able to look at striking things and marvel. Snakes are not pretty. But to the student of ethnology, especially to the student of Palestinian culture, and above all to the student of the background of that Canaanite life which resulted in a decree of capital punishment from Heaven itself, this object will be of the utmost importance. Some people are quite distressed at what they conceive to be a strange and unworthy representation of God in the decree of the extermination of the Canaanites. There are indeed persons who are horrified at the practice of most nations on earth, at the present time and in history, of putting to death notorious murderers, more, far more horrified indeed, than at the cruel and senseless murder that the criminal had committed. On the other hand people generally do not sympathize with such a view and probably never will do so in the history of the world. Righteous indignation rises in majesty and thunders the words of the Holy Writ, "Whoso sheddeth man's blood, by man shall his blood be shed." So when we get a glimpse of the practices of these Canaanites, their revolting licentiousness, their horrible child sacrifice, and the debasing character of their manner of worship, here, in fact, loathsome serpent worship, the worthiness of God's dealing with such people loses its seeming objectionable features. These people from whom comes this remarkable object, whether idol or symbol, were the Canaanites living in the land at the time the Israelites came in and were designated to be the executioners of the divine sentence.

It is difficult to discuss the genesis of such a debasing form of worship as a snake cult. The representation in so many places in the world of the tree and the serpent can hardly be accounted for by any other rational method than by supposing it in some way connected with the story of the tragedy in the Garden of Eden. Not at all that the story of the Garden suggests idolatrous worship, but that a picture of the serpent and the tree, like the sacred symbol of the crucifix which by some strange perversion of things sacred, has come, in some cases, as in Russia, to be an object of worship. Perhaps also serpent worship arose out of the idea that, since the serpent of the field had such dangerous power, it might be discreet to placate it.

It is impossible in camp to make careful researches, so that no more than suggestions can be thrown out concerning either the origin or the history of serpent worship in Palestine. It is quite possible, however, that this Canaanite idolatrous practice gave rise to the idolatrous use of the Brazen Serpent in Israel, a practice which Hezekiah suppressed.[2]

We had hurried back to camp, like a certain admiral who was absent when the battle was fought. We found that the great house in which the serpent goddess was found, had only in part been uncovered. A courtyard was in front, with apparently a stand for chariots and a feeding trough for horses. Great walls, nearly a meter thick, formed a rectangular enclosure. Within, on the first floor, was a storeroom. This room was filled on the floor space with pots for oil and wine and grain. One, at least, had in its fine flour distinctly shown in the flour charcoal remaining. In this storeroom was found the serpent goddess, which had fallen down from an upper story during the fire that consumed the building. The jars found with the stele were distinctly of the Middle Bronze Age. In that same stratum were found imitation scarabs of the Hyksos period, which would point to about the same time.

Unfortunately the excavation of this great house, whether temple or palace, is impossible this year. We must curb our impatience and wait for another season. The house is at the very edge of the section that we have been carrying down toward the bottom. To uncover all this house would require us to enlarge the area in that direction. This would not only make it necessary to begin at the top of the stratum some ten feet above us, but we have heaped upon that portion much of debris that has come out of the portion excavated, and this

---

[2] *II Kings* 18:4.

also would have to be moved again. All this would involve much work for which there is not now time left. Then, besides all this, the water in the wells is getting very low and we have to carry it for two or three miles. There have been three summers of light rainfall and the Lower Spring, from which we get our water usually, has about given out. It must be added also, that two months of the sudden and violent changes in temperature from extreme heat to unusual cold, and the strenuousness of the work is about as much as is wise at one time. We have no malaria and no mosquitoes, but sand-flies are far worse, for nothing much less than sheet iron will keep them out. There is a spraying-gun greatly recommended here. It really works like a charm — when there are no sand-flies! Altogether it is time to rest, therefore time to close our excavations and wait for another season to follow these most interesting leads.

Many other finds have been made within a few days, but have been so eclipsed by the serpent-cult object, that it seems an anti-climax to mention them now. However, the record must not neglect the little things. We have found two beautiful mace-heads, one bronze and the other diorite. The bronze one seems to have had a figure on it, but until it is cleaned of the accumulated corrosion, it is impossible to know certainly, and especially impossible to know what the figure may be. Then today a beautiful bronze dagger almost clear of rust has been found. The wooden handle has been burned away, but three of the four rivets still remain. An imitation cuneiform tablet in stone is interesting and curious, but not very valuable, as it has no inscription. It was probably a record of liver divination. It is, however, unique in Palestine, though such have been found in Syria.

A very strange, large, flat, circular stone on a foundation has excited our curiosity very much, but so far fruitlessly. The temptation to see in it an altar is very great, but the evidence seems against the idea. It seems to be in connection with an industrial plant, and, besides, there is no trace of any sacrificial use of the stone. There are no marks of fire and no indication of pouring of libations, no cup-marks as they are called, which usually occur on Canaanite altars. It is as yet a real mystery.

Fire and sword are the accompaniments of war. We have

seen and reported again and again the layers of ashes and charcoal that mark the divisions between the layers of successive cities in the *tell*. Now the horrid evidence of cruel and ruthless death in siege and destruction is furnished by the *Hakim*. Dr. Culley examined very carefully a collection of bones from the debris of the Canaanite city of about the sixteenth century, B. C., the Middle Bronze Age. Who wrought the fearful disaster we can no more than surmise. It was before the incoming of the Israelites. These bones were of both men and animals, slain in battle and burned in the fire which destroyed the city. There were bones of an old man, bones of a boy about twelve years of age, and bones of little children. None of these had been buried, all were lying face down. They had turned their faces down in agony to escape the devouring fire.

Whoever destroyed this Canaanite city was a ruthless vandal; he destroyed a culture which, though probably below the industrial development of the Judean kings, far exceeded that culture in artistic advancement: Egyptian faience, copper ingots for coinage as in the Minoan culture of Crete, furniture inlaid with ivory, the ivory in turn being itself inlaid. Here, also, is a tiny equilateral pyramid which seems to be absolutely perfect mathematically. Laid upon any one of its four sides it is still perfect. It was probably a gaming piece of some sort. It is very evident that the highest artistic culture in ancient Palestine was the early Canaanite culture. In religious ideas and life the Israelites far surpassed all others of that ancient world, but in artistic development they were far from first. This is often emphasized in both individuals and in nations in all history.

Suddenly at the end of the campaign, I had gotten money to pay the workmen and made all preparations to go down again to camp for a last journey and a last look. A call on the telephone informed me that Dr. Albright was in Jerusalem, and that everything was at a standstill. Why? That is one of the trials of the archæologist and the uncertainties of this Oriental world. Instead of an orderly finish, a sudden collapse. Such is this life of exploration. ,

It is all because of those wily sons of Esau, and we are not of the sons of Jacob to match them. Everything had moved along so pleasantly. We had given them a feast and they put in a petition that I would arrange that they be paid on Monday, May 28, as on Tuesday there would be a great Mohammedan feast and they wished the money for the feast. I had assured them that, if I could get back with the money, I would do so. Hence my preparation to go. Then some of the owners of the little garden patches on the *tell*, notably one "jail bird," who had a grudge against the chief man of his clan and was unwilling to agree with him about anything, set up the cry that we, when filling in the excavation, must put back all the debris we had taken out and every stone (!) or pay them a thousand pounds! The value of the crops raised on the land we had excavated is probably as much as two dollars a year! Such the absurdity of his claim, but absurdity does not disturb the Arab. Instance the one who refused to lend his ax "because he wanted it to shave with!" This fellow persuaded some to put in a petition to the Governor, who, to keep an appearance of fairness toward them, appointed a committee, "a senatorial investigation," to inquire into the matter, and everything stopped. When does a senatorial investigation end? Of course, the whole affair is trivial, but their scheme is to cause us delay and thereby expense in the hope that we will pay them more than is their due to get rid of them. It is another illustration of the Oriental method of annoying a prospective customer in order to make him deal with you. It is not altogether an Oriental custom either, only the Occident has more subtle ways of annoyance.

If we had money to buy the whole *tell*, we would be rid of these tricky rascals. But that we do not have. Unless they will agree to something reasonable, we will have to give up the work. Some folks think the archæologists are having a delightful jaunt abroad! The next surprise was that they had compromised their claim and had settled for *seventeen pounds, eighty-five dollars!*

There remains one thing of which our hearts are full; thanks to a gracious Providence who through storm and sunshine, over land and sea, in dust and sirocco, scorching heat and tormenting sand-flies, and in the bandit country, has ever kept us in safety and blessed us with health, given us blessed fellowship together and crowned our labors with success. The most delightful game of life is watching God's providence.

PART III

CAMPAIGN OF 1930

CHAPTER VII

CANAANITE LIFE AND RELIGION

Camp *Tell Beit Mirsim.*

THE words of the pathetic song of '63 in America, "Tenting on the Old Camp Ground," come home to us impressively this evening. The gleaming white tents on the hill were seen from afar down the valley beyond the "nether spring" on the way by which the Israelite spies came up. It is the third time we have camped here on this old threshing floor. In fact, the farmers have generously surrendered the threshing floor nearest the *tell* that we may have a high, dry and convenient camp. The kindliness of the farmers toward our work is more than matched by the delightfulness of the weather. So often have we been commiserated this spring upon the prospect of the dreadful weather of Palestine in midsummer. That we shall probably have some hot days, and maybe even hot nights, is not very alarming to folks from St. Louis and Cincinnati, and the low-lying lands of Indiana. In fact, this evening as I sit in our airy dining tent to write, I am enjoying a delightful breeze and temperature seldom equaled at any summer resort. The sky is clear, the atmosphere dry, and the gentle zephyrs from the Mediterranean make an ideal setting for our summer home, so ideal that one of the staff suggested the propriety of a contribution of one hundred dollars a week for a *delightful summer vacation.* This idyllic experience will be pleasant to recall, when some night the sand-flies invade the camp and banish sleep.

The ride down from Jerusalem, the seventy miles we are still obliged to travel to reach *Tell Beit Mirsim,* some forty miles away, was a continual delight. The green grass of spring time is all "hay cured on the ground," but the vineyards in the valley of Eshcol and all around about Hebron are prophetic of that unsurpassed lusciousness of Palestinian grapes.

"Main Street" at camp is extended to include a round dozen tents. The old *Haj,* our watchman, will have a longer beat,

137

and his little night whistle which, like the watchman's whistle in Colonial towns, announces "All's well," will need to be blown a little louder. A new cook is in the kitchen, and some new faces among the foremen from Egypt, and the staff — I must introduce them one by one, for they are to be our friends and teachers for weeks to come. The members of the principal staff are all men of doctor's degrees and all, but one, professors in theological seminaries and graduate schools, men of most serious purpose in the work of the summer that they may be thoroughly prepared as specialists to teach the Book of books (just here I had to stop and get a cap for my head because of the growing coolness toward sunset—in the *dreadful summer heat of Palestine!*).

The President of the staff is the writer, the same person as in former expeditions, but he is now Research Professor of Pittsburgh-Xenia Seminary; the Director of field operations is still Dr. W. F. Albright, now Professor of Semitic Philology in Johns Hopkins University. The expedition is a joint expedition of Pittsburgh-Xenia Seminary and the American School of Oriental Research at Jerusalem, of which Dr. C. C. McCown is now Director; he is also an *ex-officio* member of our staff. Dr. J. L. Kelso of the Department of Semitics and Archæology in Pittsburgh-Xenia Seminary is with us for a second season, a trained and expert worker; Dr. Aage Schmidt of Denmark, Assistant Director of the Danish Shiloh Expedition, is also with us for a second season and rounding out ten years of work in the excavations in Palestine. Dean J. A. Huffman of Marion Divinity School and Winona Lake School of Theology spends the first half of the season with us after some weeks in general research work throughout the land. Dr. O. R. Sellers of the Department of Hebrew and Old Testament Exegesis in the Presbyterian Seminary of Chicago. Dr. Aapeli Saarisalo of the Oriental Department of the University of Helsinki, Finland; and Dr. Nelson Glueck of the Hebrew Union College of Cincinnati, are all men of long training in Palestinian research. Even our surveyors are both trained men in such work, and our Egyptian foremen are also experienced men. We have no novices. A congenial company, perfect weather, a cordial welcome by the Arabs, old friends now, good water, and not a mosquito or sand-fly — yet. We are a happy and ardent company of explorers. Add to this that every man on the staff is a devout Old Testament student, and we set off under ideal conditions for a fruitful season of work, hard work.

And here we begin to dig. Before sun-up, Arabs were squatting around on their heels, and by half past five half a hundred of them were waiting to be enrolled for work on the *tell*. The popular opinion is that archæologists do nothing but dig up things and rejoice in their discoveries. In fact, like woodsmen clearing the land, they must spend a large part of their time clearing away the litter they make. So it is this morning; not a step of progress can we make until we clear away the house walls of the Middle Bronze Age which we left standing and move the rubbish to another place, which may later prove equally as inconvenient; and álso move the great heap of earth thrown out to the west of our excavation in 1928. We cannot put things just where we would, for the rights of property owners must carefully be respected. Good-will is a most valuable and necessary asset, and we guard it jealously.

A Circus

Just here we stop to go to the circus; not Robinson's, nor Barnum and Bailey's, nor Ringling Brothers', but something rather more unique and spectacular. There was this spring an invasion of locusts coming from the south desert, the Bedouin country. The government mobilized some two thousand five hundred of the sons of the desert to wage war on the locust. They did it successfully. As a reward for distinguished service and as an excellent opportunity to show a favor and cultivate good-will, the government arranged a great memorial celebration as a tribute to the Bedouin. It was to be a great exhibition of Bedouin riding, horse races and camel races, and all arranged at Beersheba on the edge of the desert. *Such a spectacle was not to be missed*—especially as today the diggers on the *tell* were only clearing away walls and heaps in order to begin our real work — so we determined to see the show.

We went. Some thousands of others also went, and the winds blew and the dust filled the air. Strange to say a large portion of the population of Beersheba sat in the shade at home, but the crowds from the farms on the north and from the wild desert region to the south were an amazement. It is difficult to realize that so many people live in this seemingly deserted land. For centuries, millenniums indeed, the people have had to learn concealment, so that their houses and their tents and their shelters are usually made inconspicuous, and they themselves glide along the wadies, and the traveler from abroad is apt to get the idea that few people are in the land. But this crowd spreads circle after circle from the mile-long line of tents in which the dignitaries watched the show in the shade, to the outer circle on the rim of the desert hills, where the wild men of the desert in gay-colored clothing and camel trappings looked on from afar in stately dignity. They had their own grandstand on the backs of their camels. The crowds presented the aspect of a county fair, but the setting was that of the heart of Arabia, and the west wind blew the sands like the dreaded sirocco from the desert.

I ventured near the barrier to get as good a view for a motion picture as possible. To my surprise the official photographer was a friend of mine from Jerusalem who at once asked me within the barrier to get the same views he was taking. The racing was by horsemen and camel riders in groups of four or five. First bareback riders, then men in the saddles and trappings, and then camel riders on their great lumbering beasts which run as if they were drunk; their whole gait is a series of staggers. In contrast with these was a trotting camel, a rare specimen of a most unusual riding animal. It trotted as gracefully as the easiest trotting horse. Doubtless it was the pride of its owner and would command a fabulous price.

My thoughts went back to Rephidim and the battle of Israel with the Amalekite cavalry. As fierce fighters, they are unsurpassed. One could hardly avoid a flight of imagination that saw these wild horsemen and camelmen of the desert making a strike for political freedom. They resent every attempt to impose Western ways upon them. Here was a great regiment of them gathered together, called to meet by their rulers and coming ostensibly for only peaceful sport. What if they should strike for liberty? As airplanes in ones and twos and threes circled over us, the British Tommies as well as Palestinian police moved everywhere as a part of the

HAEMATITE SEAL CYLINDER (*magnified*). THE SEAL IS ONLY AN INCH LONG AND THE
THICKNESS OF A LEAD PENCIL

(Text on page 179)

PLATE XV

spectacle, the setting for the show was only a thin, a very transparent disguise for preparedness. The whir of the air-plane propellers was a warning to any long spear of the desert with rebellion in his heart not to start anything, for bombs from the heavens might fall as fire and brimstone fell upon Sodom and Gomorrah.

But the desert contains many mysteries besides the sons of Ishmael. Look at these two owls on a stone by the roadside; the solemn, wise-looking creatures, rarely ever hooting, are the very personification of things lonesome, a living commentary on the words of the Hebrew poet, "As an owl in the desert." I recall a night at Wady Feiran, Rephidim, in 1892, sitting by the camp fire in the gloom and listening to two owls answering each other. The cook, a son of the desert, pointed to them and said, *sitt* ("lady") and *khawadjah* ("gentleman"). In the solitariness of the place, in the gloom of the night, the mournful tones of these bird lovers crooning to each other gave a most romantic touch to the words, "As an owl in the desert."

The rich valleys along the way back to camp are glowing green with the *dura,* which looks so like Indian corn, but heads out like broom corn. It is a continual wonder to people from a land of summer rains. "How," they say, "does this *dura* grow without rain?" The secret is the deep dry land planting, and then especially the dew. The Dead Sea empties iself by evaporation only; and the evaporation is condensed by the snow of Hermon and the cold upper stratum of atmosphere, and hence the dew and the crops. Providence has arranged a great evaporator and a great refrigerator, and then announced his grace "as the dew unto Israel." [1] Not until we know the land do we wholly know the Book.

Now watch your face carefully as these donkeys loaded with thorns go by us on the way, or you may be badly scratched. This is the fuel business. "The crackling of thorns under a pot," makes a furious fire, the best the desert land affords. The gathering and drying and marketing of these thorn bushes is an industrial and commercial business comparable in this land to a coal yard in America or anywhere in the British Empire. It was this secular business of a life

[1] *Hosea* 14:5.

which the man "gathering sticks" was carrying on seven days in the week in defiance of the Mosaic law for which such condign punishment was meted out to him.[2]

Just now, back at camp, as I took a siesta in the seat of the automobile, our old watchman, the *Haj,* ("pilgrim"), was taking his with a stone "for his pillow." What visions he may have had I do not know, but the vividness of the scene of that other "pilgrim," who came to Bethel and lay down with a stone for a pillow and dreamed of wondrous things, was very striking indeed. Verily, the essential customs of this land do not change very much, for they are the outgrowth of the land. Again, know the land, if you would know the Book.

Now, that much rubbish of the 1928 campaign has been cleared away, finds again begin to come out. As always here at Kirjath-sepher, they are true to type. It is still one of the strata in which cuneiform tablets are to be expected. A hundred eyes will be watching for them. In any case wondrous, interesting things will appear.

Riots and Roast Peas

I have always believed in special providences and see more and more of them as life goes on. Here is one for our work at *Tell Beit Mirsim.* When in 1929 rumors spread over Palestine inciting to riot, one of the few villages that did not respond was Dura. Its *mukhtar* was a discreet man, a grandson of Abd er-Rahman of Robinson's time, with an experience behind him of the folly and cost of riots in the days gone by. He advised the people to abide by the stuff at home until he should investigate, and then after careful inquiry he advised them to continue to abide at home and have no part in the disturbances. They heeded and so escaped the violence and death, and escaped also in large measure the aftermath of hate. "But where is the special providence?" It is impossible not to be somewhat apprehensive this year lest the hate from the riots should interfere with our work at *Tell Beit Mirsim.* This town of Dura is the home of all the farmers round about us, and of nearly *every workman employed by us.* Thus our work here, in the lov-

---

[2] *Numbers* 15:32–36.

ing-kindness of a gracious Providence, is outside the eddying currents of racial and religious animosity. Thank God!

From the Garden of Eden onward there has been that tendency to shift responsibility to the shoulders of somebody else. That is human disposition, or indisposition. Divine requirement has been, and still is—let us especially note— *still is* something very different. Cain thrust forward his "personal liberty," but the Lord held him accountable for his brother. Ezekiel unfolded in the most complete fashion the law of the Lord for watchmen; and He made every man a watchman. In Bible lands that requirement is still held to be valid. The headman of the village of *Beit Mirsim* is our night watchman. One night, while our chauffeur was away with the automobile, his tent was pilfered. The watchman is required to make good the loss. What a panic there would be among policemen and constables and United States marshals if there were such a requirement in America, or indeed anywhere among the nations who like to flatter themselves as most civilized. Then the office would, indeed, seek the man and not the man the office, and we might all sleep in peace and safety with very few bolts and bars.

The paying of the workmen, always an interesting spectacle, has increasing interest every year. At first we were obliged to pay them every week, lest they become suspicious that we would defraud them. Soon that necessity passed away. Still, pay-day was a time of restlessness among them. Now they have learned that every man's account is submitted to him and approved. They sit down in a circle and quietly wait till their names are called, and the old suspicion is almost entirely gone. They did not trust us for our Christian *profession*, but they do trust us for our Christian *living*.

Probably most people reading these accounts imagine we live in a constant environment of surprise and surpassing interest. In fact, it is only such things that I am recording. There are sometimes long stretches of desert to find a little oasis. The archæologist plods through the sand and dust and under the blazing sun that he may show others the little oasis. Today is such a stretch of sand. Some of the staff with some workmen are off on a road-making expedition in an effort to reduce the long distance to Jerusalem. The most interesting area for discovery must just now await the photographer and the surveyor, for, in scientific work, all things must be done in order. The whole work is complicated and exacting. The surveying and leveling, the drawing and photographing and recording, the provisioning of the staff of ten and the paying of a hundred employees, these things do not much interest the public, but maybe it will be of interest for a moment to know that all these things must be done by the field workers in order that others may sit at home in comfort and read of thrilling discoveries. And, in fact, I have only told you a little of the drudgery.

'Tis Independence Day, but not a holiday for us. Time is too valuable so far from home. The automobile has not yet returned from pioneering; the cook has come from a foraging expedition with some tomatoes half as big as one's hand, and has some chickens put away for evening dinner, and we are to have some firecrackers. Perhaps the neighbors will think us attacked by bandits and come to our rescue. Such is our celebration of the Fourth of July.

Now that we have completely carried the section of the mound upon which we worked in 1928 down to the bottom, surveyed and leveled, and photographed and recorded it, we have a complete conspectus of the history of the culture in the land from before 2,000 B. C. down to 600 B. C. Now we shall do at this time, what the Chinese call "taking a look see," recording briefly in rapid succession the multitude of things as they are found and the various phases of the work as they are to be seen round about the excavation and the camp.

Visitors at the camp, and, indeed, hardened archæologists themselves, are often fascinated by watching the work of the expert in fitting together potsherds and making complete pots. This man is an Egyptian of long experience and amazing skill. From a basket containing about half a bushel of scraps of pots, many of them not more than a couple of square inches in extent, and of very irregular shape, he will sort out and fit together, each in its own exact place, these little fragments, until a beautiful vase stands before us almost entirely complete. The fascination of the jig saw puzzle is as nothing to this work of reconstruction. There stands directly in front of

me at this moment a great four-handled bowl like an immense
punch bowl of elegant shape and workmanship which came
out of the diggings as a lot of apparently worthless fragments
mixed with a multitude of other fragments belonging to
other pots.

Another and totally different kind of work is being done
at the table in the reed hut used as a workshop, it is the
recording of the finds in the great book, with a carbon sheet
making a record in duplicate. Each article is drawn to exact
scale and its source and use recorded. The record has already
more than eleven hundred items, and this number will probably be increased by the close of this season to more than
fifteen hundred. This method preserves everything for the
study of the place, when the excavations have destroyed most
of the material evidence. Thus the evidence is preserved for
future generations of students. "How fascinating is the work
of the archæologist," will be the rapturous exclamation of a
reader sitting in the shade or swinging in the hammock.
Alas, the conditions under which the archæologist works do
not include hammocks in the shade, and often omit a great
many things usually considered matters of course at home.
If here you enter a grocery or an optical instrument store or
a jeweler's to have a typewriter repaired, and ask, "When will
these things be ready?" the answer is, "Oh, such a time —
any time you wish." You go away rejoicing and in hope, only
to find that nothing is done until you come again. The practical maxim of the Orient is, "Never do anything now that
can be put off to a later time."

Gruesome things are sometimes found, as the snake goddess
in 1928 and now the goddess of childbirth. This latter was
also Canaanite, but, alas, comes from a section of the Israelite
occupation of the city, another piece of material evidence of
the truth of the constant charge of Israel's prophets and re-
formers that the people fell into the idolatry and superstition
of the land.

Sickles are frequently found in every level like this one from
soon after the time of Solomon and this other from about the
time of Saul. Sickles vary somewhat in shape, but are all
sickles. A plowshare from the time of the Judges is much
like those in use here in all ages down to the present time.

This one is of iron, as is also a small axe-head from the same period, as well as a large and beautiful bronze axe. Bronze did not entirely cease to be used when iron became predominant. Especially there was that time in the period of the Judges when the Philistines, who introduced iron smelting, tried to hold on to a monopoly of the iron business, and the Israelites were obliged to go to the Philistine smithies to have the mattock and the coulter sharpened. Are these relics memorials of that time? Perhaps so. Arrowheads in both iron and bronze also come from the Israelite period. Slingstones, usually of flint, are very common in all ages; we get bushels of them, especially around the walls. This fine large one of flint beautifully made is about the size of a ten-pound cannon ball. I think it would feel very much like one on a man's head. This little bronze bracelet was the delight of some child about the time of David, and likewise this little decorated ivory pendant for a necklace. These beautifully shaped stone buttons and tiny beads from the Canaanite period are pathetic memorials of the never-failing feminine love of ornament.

We have not found many stairways. There was one fine stairway to an upper story coming from about the time of Hezekiah. We find now two winding stairs. One of them is back in a portion of the "C" level, that is the city of the Canaanites destroyed by Israel, where it gave access to the bottom of a grain pit; the other is a much larger stairway of the city first built by the Israelites ("B" level), when they came in. At one point they made a cellar by building down into the debris of the city they had destroyed, constructing a winding stair to this cellar.

This mountain was a good watch tower. In the Canaanite tongue, which Hebrew was, it was a *migdal*. It occupied a site on this mountain top which seemed to block the valleys. In the picturesque language of the Orient, it reached up to heaven; for the clouds often rested on the top of it. It was a good place to fortify for defense, and so they made houses with strong walls and a great door, so that each house was its own defense. Such a specially constructed house was found at this level in the debris of the city, the great court still intact.

One thing has always been lacking in our finds here; in all the Israelite period there have been found few and very small door-sockets; the people seem to have used only light wooden doors or curtains. Later, however, away back in the middle of the Canaanite period, several sockets were found, but not in place. Now at last, we have found a beautiful great one *in situ*. It belongs to this troubled period of turmoil and transition at the beginning of Hyksos times. What significance is evident in door-sockets being found only at that period? That great door-socket in its place in a heavy wall gave the whole construction a fortress-like appearance. It had the appearance of an Oriental caravansary and quite probably was such. But when the whole outline of this court of the caravansary was cleared of rubbish, at once another and much earlier similarity suggested itself to us. We immediately declared this to be an Abrahamic house. Why? Do you not remember the story of Lot and the angel messengers who came to warn him? The angels proposed to stay in the street for the night. Lot said "No." He knew the people of Sodom and would not allow his guests to be subjected to the dangers of a night on the street. He insisted that they come into his house for protection. They came; the mob also came, came and battered at the door, but they did not get in. His house had a door strong enough to resist a mob. Here is a very graphic revelation of the sociological and political conditions of life at Sodom in that day. Violence was rampant; police protection was not very good. The house of a rich man like Lot must be his castle, strong enough to resist a mob.

So when we saw this court of the caravansary at Kirjath-sepher with its great heavy walls and its giant door-socket, eight inches in diameter, we said at once, "This is an Abrahamic house." This door-socket carried a door strong enough to resist a mob and was set in a wall heavy enough for a castle. But was it of that age? *Exactly so.* So important a piece of evidence as that was not overlooked. This level is that of the transitional period between the Middle Bronze Age and the Early Bronze Age that preceded it. The pottery is that strange mixture of Early Bronze and Middle Bronze found at the temple of Ader at the beginning of the civilization of Moab in the days of Lot. The degenerated ledge handles of that transition were especially prominent here. Here was unmistakably the civilization of the time of

Abram and Lot. The same sociological and political conditions prevailed. The pottery had added the realistic touch to the account of Lot and the Angels which marks it as a contemporaneous narrative. We seemed to be transported over the stretch of 4,000 years and to stand in the streets of Sodom as Lot said, "Come into my house." Here we found a brazier with the roasted chick peas of someone's dinner still in the receptacle. A dish of peas prepared 4,000 years ago and served today at *Tell Beit Mirsim!* Will so much of our civilization be obtainable 4,000 years hence?

The chick peas roasted four thousand years ago are now joined on our archæological table by some fresher parched wheat which has been cooked only about three thousand years, coming as it does from another section of the *tell* from about the time of Hezekiah or somewhat later. In this court was also a place for the feeding of horses, which adds another element to the appearance of a caravansary, a place of public entertainment where men and beasts camped down together. Such places of public entertainment continued down until a quarter of a century ago and are perhaps still found in places. This is exactly such a place as the stable in which our Lord was born.

CHAPTER VIII

THE FEUDAL AGE IN PALESTINE

Camp *Tell Beit Mirsim.*

THERE are two plagues of camp life in Palestine. One is dust that gets on everything and into everything and fills one's nose and eyes and gets between one's teeth. The other is — worse! Palestine is a land of bugs, and beetles, and moths, and insects, and scorpions, and snakes, about everything that flies, or flits, or creeps, or crawls, or wriggles, *and bites.* Of an evening around the big lamp in the dining tent, one might make a collection of flying, buzzing things that creep and crawl over one's hands and face, and sometimes bite or sting, that would make a professional entomologist wild with delight. It is a paradise of "bugs." Then one's imagination gets to work until it seems as though, when anything touches one anywhere, it is a new kind of bite!

Then there is the weather, — more weather than anywhere else in the world. Palestine is beautifully said by commentators to exemplify all climes from the frigid zone in the snow-cap of Hermon to the torrid belt at the low level of the Dead Sea twelve hundred and fifty feet below sea level, with all the varieties in between. It may equally, but more prosaically, be said that Palestine has all kinds of weather and has them all the time.

The early morning of a new day! This is another of the beauties and delights of our patriarchal existence. The clouds upon which we have looked are but the shadows that form the background against which are laid the bright colors of the picture. Of these none are more pleasing than the sunrises and the sunsets. The beauties of nature are, indeed, lavished upon Palestine. Everywhere we find beauty and stones. The Arabs have a legend that the angel Gabriel was given two bags of stones for the whole world. He dropped one bag in Palestine, and so had only one bag left for all the rest of the

149

world. But if it is a stony land, it is also a land of most wonderful beauty of flowers and skies and twilights.

Then is anything else so refreshing in a dry hot land as a deep drink of sweet water from a great spring? Our water carrier is that little donkey with wooden saddlebags made to hold four Standard Oil gasoline tins of five gallons each, twenty gallons in all. Four or five times a day he makes the journey, a mile and back, to the "nether spring" to bring us the cool, delicious water from its depths. On a still day we can hear the "song of the well" as the shepherds draw water for the flocks and herds that come to the troughs to drink. Do we get ice to keep the water cool? Not so! The Orient knows a better way. They make in Egypt that porous water bottle which permits the water to filter very slowly through to a saucer in which the bottle stands. This bottle, set in the wind, cools the water by evaporation, and the hotter the day, and the drier the sirocco, the cooler is the water.

And music! We are even not without music, seemingly the only original jazz band. There is a long-necked, pumpkin-like banjo, a pipe that surely might be the father of all saxophones, and a drum that would delight a Navajo medicine man. Neither do the players forget to hold out their hands in true Italian hotel style. Oh, we are quite up-to-date in the matter of entertainment in the wilderness. Incidentally, the bag-pipes have completely captured the imagination of the Arabs. They think "the pipes noo" are the ideal of all good music. Their tunelessness does actually suit the Arab disposition to improvise without troubling himself about a melody.

But there are so many things wise and otherwise in the desert life that I hardly know where to begin. One might write a long chapter on the dust and certainly not exhaust the dust, but that does not end the matter. The archæologist is a man who dusts things; yes, literally. In the evening, when the workmen have done their "eight hours" and have gone wearily home, perhaps to work two or three hours more in the harvest field, the archæologist sits down to twenty, thirty, even forty baskets of potsherds all to be examined and brushed or washed to determine exactly the history revealed by the day's work. It is like house cleaning every day in the week, week after week. Occasionally grotesque and laughable decorations appear; whether they are the work of some

old-time burlesque cartoonist and the decoration of the potsherds was their way of putting out the comic page of their
newspaper, we do not know, but this forenoon there came in
from the expert who puts together the fragments two pieces
of what is called Philistine pottery, because similar to Philistine decoration, making a remarkably grotesque creature. The
staff is divided in opinion as to whether it is a bird or an
animal. It seems to have the legs of an animal, the toes of a
bird, the head and crest and the wattles of a big bird, but the
afterpart of the creature is wanting, so that it is quite impossible to say whether or not it had a tail and some other legs
at the other end. The creature is evidently running from
something behind it of which it is afraid and against which
it is very angry; for its head is turned around over its back
and its beak is wide open as though it were screaming. The
description may sound like the description of the work of
some child or of some ignoramus; but it is not so. There is a
marked element of grotesquerie in the drawing which shows
the skill of a real cartoonist. It is a genuine comic cartoon
placed as decoration on a piece of pottery. Perhaps it does
not reflect any more of the civilization or the moral character
of the Israelites of the time of the Judges, from which period
it comes, than does the comic page of the daily newspaper
reflect real American life.

Many limestone basins are found in the rooms of the houses,
particularly in the Israelite period, though not exclusively so.
Perhaps it is because we have more of the remains of the
Israelite period than of the Canaanite that they seem more
numerous. Some of these basins are of a hard, refractory
limestone, not easily calcined. These were suitable for fire-
pots for cooking purposes, and evidently were so used. They
are much blackened inside by the action of the fire. Other
basins are of the beautiful white limestone, which takes a
polish very like marble and is very susceptible to the influence
of fire. No fire has been used in them. They are not blackened or calcined. We can only imagine the use to which they
were put, possibly for ablutions, almost certainly as receptacles
in which to wash things, and doubtless also for the mixing
of food.

It was reported earlier in our work of excavation here that
these old cities had no street cleaning department, that they

permitted the rubbish to accumulate in the streets and if, in time, the street became too high for the threshold of the house they could make steps up to the street, as we sometimes find in modern Jerusalem homes, and as we found also here in 1928. Or, in case they did not wish to do that — well, they could put in a new floor and raise the roof. In our work this afternoon we have found a portion of the city of the kings of Judah where they *actually pursued this latter method.* At least, they put in a new threshold, which is still *in situ,* and if it made the ceiling so low that they would bump their heads, they would surely raise the roof. As Nebuchadnezzar destroyed all these roofs, that part of the alteration cannot now be seen.

Come with me for a look about the workshop, which is in fact a reed hut constructed as a shelter for the work of the photographer and recorder, and as a storehouse for the finds. Note these great feast bowls, in size and shape like a great chinaware punch bowl, a very great one, in fact. They come from the times of the kings of Judah, the best period of Israelite history. These bowls were too large for family use. They were undoubtedly for the purpose of social entertainment. It would be an exaggeration to say that one is found in every house, but they are very numerous indeed. In them was placed probably the whole of a roasted kid or lamb, and about it gathered the whole company at the feast. They have three, sometimes four, handles, and are occasionally quite beautifully decorated by the ring burnishing over a red slip placed on the pottery, which makes the whole inside of the bowl a set of concentric pink rings. Then these black cooking pots were even more essential to the culinary department of an Israelite home. Some of them are quite large, for the cooking of a great dinner. Most of them are what might be called strictly family size, but here are two tiny little cooking pots that have been very much used, deeply blackened over the fire. One is puzzled to know to what use were put the very small ones, unless they were for the amusement of the daughters while they learned to cook.

Then note these scores of little juglets with the pinched lip at the top for the pouring out of the various unguents that were placed in them. Most valuable of all because of its rarity here at Kirjath-sepher and its uniqueness anywhere, is this flat, open top bowl from the time of the Judges. Its peculiarity is that it has a small handle on the side, as for pouring, and a rather capacious spout projecting on the other side. It was not a cooking pot and apparently was used for some liquid. Perhaps it was a soup dish. One might think of the pottage that Esau so longed for when he was famished.

Now the journey to Jerusalem must be made again for provisions to feed a hungry staff and money to satisfy the longing of the workmen for their wages. We do not say much about the dangers of the life that we live; but perhaps the picture would not be complete, as no picture is, without some of the shadows. There is far less banditry in this land than in our boastful America, yet we always live in the shadow of possible bandit raids. We are very careful to pay every man in the work all that is due him, but we are equally careful that it does not become known just when he is going to get it, and so pay day is moved about. Sometimes it is delayed and sometimes it is moved forward a day or two, and thus that meddlesome old hag, Dame Rumor, cannot inform any would-be Palestinian gangsters when we are likely to be coming down from Jerusalem with the money, and we are very careful not to keep the money overnight in the camp.

Then, with all the precautions that we can take for health and the prevention of any sort of contagion, the incorrigible disposition of the Arabs to be utterly regardless of any precautions for safety in the handling of water or food constitutes a constant menace to health. If visitors who come to the camp, perhaps even members of the staff, knew always all that is to be seen around the place, they would live in constant aversion and dread. But the archæologist who always plays safe will never be an archæologist.

A Mystery Building

Here we begin the record of the last week of this season of work. It begins with great anticipations. We have pushed diligently forward with the excavations in order to reach that level in the ruins to which belongs the palace or temple from which came the great Canaanite idol two years ago. At the end of last week, part of the outline of that building appeared in the level of the Middle Bronze Age which we had just reached, and now at the beginning of this week everybody on the staff, and the foreman on the *tell,* and even some of the workmen are very much excited and on the alert for everything that will inform us of that building. We are not exactly picking out the walls with a toothpick, but we do use a small trowel and a brush, lest we may destroy some fresco or some other interesting relic. Day by day I will record our progress and the realization of our hope — or disappointment! We shall hope it will not be disappointment.

"The things that men do live after them," is a very trite saying, but it is by the realization of this fact that our archæological work succeeds. The things that men did of old in erecting their own homes, in making great temples, in waging wars, in burning cities, all these things "live after them," and by these things we learn what they did. This moralizing may be of some value in a general way, but I have indulged in it in order to bring you a very practical and rather startling illustration. This rough, broken, hollow piece of pottery which one of the draftsmen is recording was a mold made in soft clay and then baked, made for the purpose of casting images of the Canaanite goddess of birth. The potter, in making that mold, carefully manipulated the clay with his thumb and fingers. He did it so delicately that he left perfect imprints of his finger marks. They were burned in the furnace. Doubtless the mold was used many times and, after lying in the ruins for thousands of years, now is dug up to show to the world, and we have the *finger prints of that old potter* as accurately recorded as the finger prints of any criminal laid up in the records of a police station. A solemn thought, that all the impressions we make in this world, all the "finger prints" of our conduct, abide. Future generations may read them and the recording angel has them all down in his book.

Now you are all impatient to know about the coming out of that temple or palace. Well, it is coming out, and that is almost as much as we can say yet. It is a curious ruin, quite different from the other houses around, and with pick and hoe and basket and small trowel and sieve we are raking and shaking the dust of that old palace every moment in hope of finding some interesting trinket or some important cult object or, best of all, an archive, a pot of tablets; but — we may not get anything. This town has been called "Book Town." There may be books here or there may not be books here; but the town itself is the principal book that is here. The pages of that book we have turned one by one and they are telling us the whole story of civilization in this land for a period of nearly, if not quite, two thousand years, one of the most important periods also in the history of this land. Whatever the temple or palace may prove to be, it will, after all, be but an illustration like a woodcut or a fine steel engraving that illustrates the *book which the city is.*

We must still call the mystery building by the Egyptian name "The Great House"; we are not able yet to know certainly whether it was a palace or a temple. Onc thing is certain; it has been ruthlessly pillaged as it would be in either case, whether palace or temple. Still some cult objects probably would not be carried away, if it were a temple, and these will ultimately decide the question. A storeroom next to that in which we found the Canaanite idol in 1928 is being emptied. In the bottom is a mass of crushed pottery. Among this we may find some things that the looters did not carry away. One of the most interesting things in all the work of excavation is the careful scraping out of a place like this by the foreman and some of the skilled workmen in addition to some of the members of the staff. The utmost care is exercised that nothing escapes detection. The workmen have caught the spirit of curiosity seekers and so lynx-eyed are they that, although in the last two days we have put twenty-five bushels of debris through the sieve, the sifters caught nothing that the diggers had passed, except two little Babylonian hematite weights. I say Babylonian, for this building belongs to the Middle Bronze Age, which, although politically subject to Egypt most of the time, still retained the Babylonian culture of the preceding age. That culture lasted a long time, as most distinctly certified by the *Tell el-Amarna* tablets, which still at the date of the late Eighteenth Dynasty of Egypt, the time of Akhenaton, were written in the cuneiform script and in the Babylonian tongue of a Palestinian dialect.

Yesterday evening I must needs go to Jerusalem to get more money to pay more men for doing more work. That is the routine here. And carrying money through the bandit country is beginning to get a little bit on my nerves. However, like the fear of ghosts, this is probably a ghostly fear. Nevertheless a real bandit is no ghost whether in Chicago or in southern Palestine. We started away from the camp when the temperature was ninety-eight in the shade; there was such a delightful cool breeze blowing in from the sea that we certainly had not suffered from the heat; but alas, when we reached the Beersheba road and started across the plain toward the hill country of Judea the air was so hot it was difficult to keep one's eyes open. It felt as though we were passing in front of a furnace; but we consoled ourselves with the thought that when we got up on the mountain it would be cool. Alas! For a little while it was cool and then it got hotter. When we reached Jerusalem we found that the temperature for the day was 108°.

And now what about that palace or temple? That is just what we should like to know. It is impossible yet to know, and probably we shall never know, whether it was a palace or a temple; but it was a great building on a grand scale with heavy walls and evidences of there having been elegance in it at some time. But completely pillaged! Some beautiful inlay work was found, indicating elegant furniture, and while the Canaanite goddess came out of this building, seemingly we found no other evidence of any religious character to the place. We found a very beautiful Hyksos scarab which accords with the age to which it belongs and is correct enough historically. A sidelight on the morals or the dissipation that went with the place was a *rather elegant set of dice*. Whether palace or temple, it seems in any case to have been a gambling den.

At the very last some important historical object may yet appear; but it looks now as if we should be content with the book *that the city is*.

We began this evening to transport the antiquities to Jerusalem for division by the Department of Antiquities when the portion left to us will be packed and shipped home to Pittsburgh-Xenia Seminary. Next week we will clear up the surface of the *tell*, settle up with the owners of the ground, break up camp, and go home.

THE FEAST

The last great event of our camp experiences of 1930 was the usual feast, not another example of Arab hospitality, but a response in kind. There was a tent for *mukhtars,* a carpeted and cushioned tent. The men sat down in groups, and the boys in other little companies, one hundred and ten in all. They sat down, not on the green grass, like the thousands at Bethsaida, for there is no grass here at this season of the year, but they squatted on the bare dusty ground in the sun (for it proved a very cool day), and then a row of dusky hands plunged into those platters, and the mutton and rice disappeared with incredible swiftness; the one who could eat the fastest got the most. With so great a company, it was impossible to serve them as elaborately as they sometimes served us; but they have worked faithfully and pleasantly; we have had no trouble whatever; and we would not be outdone by these humble folk of the wilderness in the finer qualities of courtesy and hospitality. The Arab has a sweet tooth, so a big bag of candies, such as he likes, was brought from Jerusalem, and they were soon put where they tasted best. The feast was over, and the company trooped away home as happy as children who had been to a picnic. The fete cost a goodish bit of good money, but the best things of life usually come high, and will come only to those who pay the price.

PART IV

CAMPAIGN OF 1932

CHAPTER IX

PATRIARCHS AND FEUDAL LORDS

LEVELS "E," "F," "G," "H," "I," "J"

Camp Tell Beit Mirsim.

THE afternoon was bright and warm, even hot, though the rapid movement of the car made, at times, a pleasant breeze and, at times, confronted us with a hot breath, as though a blast from a furnace. It was mid-afternoon, just the time when the "wind of evening" begins to have more of the tang of the sea. We had set out for a two hours' run to Jerusalem for provisions for twelve men who live in the open, and have real appetites; a journey and an errand which we have to make about three times every week. We rushed rapidly down the camel trail, past the "nether spring," across the stony way and up the still stonier slope and had topped the hill for the long run down to the Hebron-Beersheba road.

Up that long slope came a strange cavalcade, strange to all who do not know the desert and its ways. Thousands of goats and sheep spread over the yellow fields on either side of the trail searching for every scrap of fodder that even a goat can eat. Nearer the well-beaten trail were hundreds of camels, great shaggy, solemn, and supercilious camels, young sleek and trim half-grown camels, and spindle-legged awkward camel colts. The pack camels were laden with the most heterogeneous collection of domestic paraphernalia imaginable, ofttimes topped with a woman and two or three babies. People there were also, many people, walking along the way; strong stalwart men and women walking with vigor, not the listless, hopeless air of tramps and vagabonds, but with the look rather that is attributed to the pioneers of empire striding forward to fortune. One great caravan succeeded another until it seemed as if the desert of Sinai was emptying itself into the Negeb, and pushing north to the Shephelah. Exactly that was what we were seeing. The desert was emptying itself of its inhabitants, in search for food and water. They were not hysterical because of the hard conditions of life; they were not calling upon the government to give them a hand-out, or passing resolutions that somebody must do something about it. They were meeting the situation by a readjustment, and they did it with their heads up and their look forward and the light of hope, the hope of determination, in their eyes.

What did it all mean? "There was famine in the land." So it was in the days of Abram, and so in the days of Jacob, and so now. A scarcity of water is always a famine in this land. The people live very simply at all times, and in times of famine always very close to the borderline of destitution. Food and drink they must have to live, and if these are found even in meager supply, they hope for tomorrow; "inshalla." These hosts came into a land parched and bare, yet there is no outcry, no forbidding barrier set up to keep the needy out. People share with them and with their flocks; they move on to other pastures as did the sons of Jacob, when Joseph, the young sheikh in his new ceremonial coat, the insignia of his office, went to bring their report.

But what has all this to do with Biblical archæology at Kirjath-sepher? It has much to do with it this season. In nearly the whole of this campaign our work is in the Patriarchal Period, the Bronze Ages, the Canaanite life in the land. It was among these very Canaanites from the end of the Early Bronze Age onward to the close of Late Bronze that the Patriarchs lived and moved about on their various journeys, when there was "famine in the land." When they moved, did they look like these caravans which we have just met trekking northward? Undoubtedly! The Patriarchs were Bedouin princes, with just such a retinue of sheep and goats and camels and families and dogs, and the life they lived was of the culture of the land which we are digging up day by day. Does it seem impossible to talk of culture among such a motley company as we have met on the way? What is culture? The story of these Ages so clearly outlined in the debris at *Tell Beit Mirsim* will well answer our questions.

So "there was a famine in the land"; and there is now. It may not be as severe as in the days of Abram, probably is not. Certainly it is not as in the days of Joseph, when "the famine was over all the face of the earth." One begins to wonder if

that may happen again! Will the problems of over-produc-
tion and over-population be thus solved in the future as in
the past?

Be that as it may be in the all-wise providence of God,
there is now "a famine in the land." As we came down the
familiar road from Jerusalem to camp we found that we
were like the Psalmist, "in a dry and thirsty land." The
information at Jerusalem that the rainfall was very much
below the usual was disconcerting, but the parched appearance of the little fields among the stones, the half-withered
leaves of the trees, the dried-up appearance of even the world-
famous Vale of Mamre, brought home to us the tragic significance that "a famine was in the land." Then, when we
dropped down from Dhahariyeh to the Plain of Beersheba,
the bare harvest fields, the forsaken threshing-floors, and the
unplanted dura fields, usually at this season waving green
like an American cornfield in July, filled us with dismay. Must
we bring water twenty-two miles from Abraham's well at
Beersheba. or should we really be able to proceed at all with
the excavations this year, or be obliged to return home empty-
handed? The black tents of the Bedouin in the yellow barren
fields looked like remnants of a vanished race in a devastated
world. A few peasants were drawing up the driblets of the
"nether spring" from which we have been accustomed to
bring our water, but which we must now leave to the thirsty
villagers. The money we bring into the community as wages
is a bright hope to them, but we must not rob them of their
last drink of water. Present-day experiences here certainly
illustrate the Biblical record, "a famine was in the land."

A little inquiry enables us to buy water from a large cistern near by. Filtered and boiled and then cooled in Egyptian porous water bottles, it has given us excellent, cool, soft
drinking water. Men and boys flocked to work for us, gathering about the camp at four o'clock in the morning to get a
job. A large and most congenial staff assembled; our old
cook, Isa, was in the kitchen, our old chauffeur at the
wheel, and our most competent Egyptian foremen were on
the *tell* and, despite the drought, camp life soon began to
move smoothly in the old grooves. Such are the ways of
Providence: "Weeping may endure for a night, but joy
cometh in the morning."

Thus first the illustration of Palestinian life in one of its most tragic moods; now the announcement of the special theme of the fourth campaign at *Tell Beit Mirsim*, the ancient Kirjath-sepher, and the theme also for the climax of all our campaigns here: — The Culture of Bible Lands, the Matrix of Bible Narratives. Here, as we have been seeing, is the matrix into which true narratives must fit, whether we inspect the matrix in the ruins of some *tell*, of an ancient city, or find it in the experiences of the land and the persistent customs of the people; the culture of Bible lands did not terminate with the end of revelation, but lives in the land and the life lived here. For the most part, illustrations of that culture will be drawn from the work at old Kirjath-sepher, but ever joined most intimately with the same culture elsewhere, and also now as well as in ancient times. Life is ever a continuum, and cannot correctly be understood from fragments broken off at some date, as though Providence and nature respected our little artificial schedules. Tomorrow is only the continuation of today.

STAFF AND ORGANIZATION

There was a time when almost any one could get a permit to dig and do the work in the way that pleased himself and promised the most immediate spectacular returns — if he had patience enough and money enough to secure the firman from the Turkish government. Such were the conditions in Palestine, and, indeed, they were much the same in Egypt and in Asia Minor and the Euphrates valley; for once Turkey controlled all of Bible lands. Now all, or nearly all, is changed. Turkey controls, of Bible lands, only Asia Minor. All the remainder is directly or indirectly in Christian hands. While, if an applicant for permit to excavate has the proper qualifications, there is no delay and the cost is little or nothing, yet governmental requirements are very severe, though reasonable, and founded upon the soundest principles, both mandatory and restrictive; many things are specifically required and not a few specifically forbidden, and many restrictions have been recently added. Thus it becomes of the utmost importance to do all things in the way laid down in the government requirements, of which more particularly presently. To the end of carrying out these rigid requirements,

the staff and the organization, the individual qualifications
of the members of the staff and the division of labor among
the members is a matter of prime interest to us and importance to the public. Upon these ends and another special
end of our own, depends the ultimate value of our work. It
is quite possible to spend a great deal of money, turn over a
vast amount of debris and actually bring to light many valuable individual objects to very little purpose (except personal
glorification) and at the same time destroy forever the opportunity for better work to be done at that place. The treasure-
hunters and dealers in antiquities may do all this at no cost
to the public and quite a profit to themselves. Not a little so-
called archæological work in the past, and some in the not
very distant past, has also been of this same character. Our
aim and the aim of most workers in the field today, is to
carry out most sedulously the requirements of the Antiquities
Department. To this end, the personnel and organization of
the staff are given most careful consideration.

The work this year, as in the 1930 campaign, is a joint
expedition of Pittsburgh-Xenia Seminary and the American
School of Oriental Research in Jerusalem, both institutions
being sources of funds and equipment in about equal amounts.
Pittsburgh-Xenia contributes the President of the staff, Dr.
Melvin Grove Kyle, and Johns Hopkins University, the Director
of Field Operations, Dr. William F. Albright, who after this
year will resume again also his place as Director of the Ameri-
can School in Jerusalem. This year Dr. Nelson Glueck of
Hebrew Union College, Cincinnati, is Director of the American
School and, as such, *ex-officio,* a member of the staff at
Tell Beit Mirsim. It has been especially helpful that it has
been possible for him to be actually present in the work a
large part of the season. Dr. James L. Kelso of Pittsburgh-
Xenia Seminary, Professor of Semitics and Archæology, is
Assistant to the Director. In addition, we have again Dr. Aage
Schmidt of the Danish Shiloh Expedition; Dr. Cyrus Gordon,
Fellow of the American School of Oriental Research in Bagh-
dad; Mr. Henry Detweiler, Architect; Dr. W. F. Stinespring,
Fellow of Yale University; the Reverend Eugene Liggitt, Fel-
low of Pittsburgh-Xenia Seminary; the Reverend John Bright,
Associate Professor of Hebrew in Union Seminary, Richmond,
Va.; the Reverend Vernon Broyles, Fellow of Union Seminary,

Richmond, Va.; Mr. Stephen N. Reynolds, student of Princeton Seminary, and Mr. William Gad, of Assiut, Egypt,surveyor. As in every campaign, the consulting members of the staff are Père Vincent of the French School in Jerusalem, and Dr. Clarence Fisher, Professor of Archæology in the American School in Jerusalem. The efficiency and sufficiency of such a staff might be adequately indicated by the individual mention of them just made, and will be still more manifest by a statement of the organization and the wider scope of intention in the organization and the work.

A large and effective personnel on the staff is not of itself enough; there must be an equally effective organization. This organization we have been perfecting, campaign by campaign, until it has now reached a high degree of efficiency. We will not say it will never be improved, but we make every improvement possible each campaign. In the management of the expeditions, there is a very sharp, clear division of duties and responsibilities; a most necessary thing not only to effectiveness of the work, but to the satisfaction of the workers and to unbroken harmony. The President of the staff presides at all its meetings, supervises the general welfare of the staff and the men on the *tell,* coördinates all the departments of the work and secures complete coöperation everywhere; directs publicity concerning the work during its progress, keeping the public informed through the daily press, the weekly religious press, and quarterly magazines, and especially on the lecture platform in colleges, universities, and theological seminaries in America and in the mission fields.

The Director of Field Operations is very exactly what his title indicates. He directs all the work of the expedition; the foremen on the *tell,* and all the other members of the staff, as well, obey his orders and, with the aid of his assistant and the various members of the staff and the foremen, the work is so systematized that it goes forward as smoothly as the work in the present-day great industrial establishments. The Director also prepares the technical record of all the work for the *Bulletin of the American School of Oriental Research* and for the *Annual* published by them.

The duties of the various members of the staff are also equally systematically arranged. Assignments are made in such fashion that, consistent as far as possible with the special qualifications of each member of the staff, each one shall have as varied a part in the work as will give him the widest knowledge of archæological research.   There is much work to be done on the *tell*, as some members of the staff are required to be there all the time to assist the foremen; and, in addition to surveying and keeping the records and photographing all the materials, there is a vast work of recording and drawing even the tiniest fragment that comes out of the ruins so that each member of the staff, as far as possible, is given part time at work at the table in the tent and part time work on the *tell*, to learn as much as possible of all the technicalities involved.   Naturally, also, such an arrangement contributes to the health and the comfort, as well as the acquisition of knowledge, of each member of the staff.   Too long a stay on the *tell*, when the direct heat of the sun is anywhere from 110 to 150 degrees, is very exhausting; then two or three hours' quiet work in the tent with a cool sea breeze blowing is restful and invigorating.

These plans for carrying on the work have grown up and have been corrected and improved year by year and embodied in a set of regulations, rules, if you wish so to call them.   It is usual to give each member of the staff a copy of the regulations, but this year the President of the staff was a little late in arriving and found everything working so smoothly and harmoniously and according to rule, that he found it unnecessary to distribute the regulations.

Now all this elaborate preparation for order and system is to an end, not simply the obvious end of order and system, but to a far more important and purposeful intent.   A little history of religious movements since the Reformation will make plain not only our intent, but the use which it may serve.   Immediately after the Reformation and indeed the motive power of it, Theology was the master director of all Biblical interpretation, and the theologian was the field marshal of religion in those turbulent days; then, when he seemed to have command of the field, a rival showed his head above the horizon and at not too distant a date not only became a colleague, but disputed the supreme command with the theologian.   This rival was Criticism, textual, literary, and historical.   Then, for a long time and until recently, within a **quarter** of a century, Theology and Criticism have **directed,**

and assumed the exclusive right to direct, all Biblical interpretation and hence all Biblical religious ideas. But a third
aspirant won a place in the field of interpretation about a
quarter of a century ago, and has rapidly pushed forward to
an equal place in interpretation, if not indeed the supreme
place. This third aspirant is thorough Scientific Research
in Bible lands to lay alongside of the Biblical record the material remains of the culture of Bible lands to see how they
compare, on the principle that the culture of Bible lands is
the matrix of Bible narratives. If the narratives be correct,
they must inevitably, indeed necessarily, fit the matrix. Such
Archæological Research has rapidly pushed forward to an
equal place in Biblical interpretation with Theology and Criticism and, from the very essentials of the material, is boldly
challenging for the first place; *for facts are final.* Theology
proclaims a message of God to the world; Criticism assigns
the sacred documents to their place in literature; Archæology
discovers the setting of the message in history. If the message were not worthy, it could not be from God; if the documents be not genuine, then the message must be a forgery;
and if the events of the message had no place in history, the
message itself would be a delusion.

Now, if the teachers and preachers of the Gospel are to be
real Bible interpreters they must be familiar with the message of this new leader. It will not be enough that they read
everything coming from the press and keep abreast of current
events or that they know all the helpfulness and all the vag-
aries of criticism and are familiar with all the profundities
of theology, whether of the metaphysical realism of the
Middle Ages or the unfettered reasoning of the pragmatist
from the days of Bacon onward, but they must know just
what the Biblical writers meant when they wrote under the
influence of the language and the manners and customs and
the imagery of their own times; in short, to be Biblical interpreters they must know the life that molded and gave
expression to the thoughts of the Biblical writers. They must
know the life of the Orient as Moses and Samuel and Ezekiel
knew it, yes, and also as it is today; for life is a continuum,
no one can draw a line anywhere, as some have tried to do,
and say here the ancient life ceased and modern life began.
The human race is the same in all ages, the same in its in-

stincts, its intuitions and its physical senses. It lives on and on, and as the geography and environment are still the same as in Bible times, very much of the life of Bible times is still lived in Bible lands, and no one thoroughly knows the Bible to interpret it to others who does not know that life.

So, the religious and educational intent of our carefully elaborated organization and method for archæological excavation is to bring year by year to our staff, men from the various theological institutions of the world, especially from the Old Testament departments, and from the New Testament departments; and give them such an insight into every part of the work and the reliability of its conclusions that in their several places they shall pass on to the coming generations of preachers of the Word, all over the world, correct ideas of Biblical interpretation, and necessarily and certainly inspire their pupils with an imperative desire to know Bible lands for themselves. Thus the plans of Dr. Albright and myself year by year are not simply to get the facts in the field, but through these members of the staff to pass on those facts in such a way as to determine Biblical interpretation for the future.

EXCAVATIONS AND DISCOVERIES

The excavations of 1932 began exactly where the work of 1930 left off. It was the Canaanite period of the Late Bronze Age, at the end of the "C" level at *Tell Beit Mirsim*. At the time we found the sculptured lion, one front paw was missing. Strange to say (one of the unexpected happenings in archæological work) at the very outset of our work this year we found that missing paw and sent it up to the museum in Jerusalem.

I have referred in the introduction to the method as well as to the organization of our work. The method, the requirement of the Department of Antinquities, and indeed, the only scientific method, is, in all our work, to remove the ruins of the *tell* layer by layer. In speaking of these layers as levels it must not be understood that they are at all times at the same altitude above sea level. The top of the mountain was irregular, there are high and low places, and not every city built on this mountain, perhaps not any one of the cities, covered the whole surface within the walls. Thus the levels

denominated as "A," "B," "C," and so forth, mark the remains of the successive cities as now separated by indubitable
traces of the conflagration that destroyed each city. Moreover, it would be quite impossible to carry on the work by
removing each level, that is, the ruin of each city, throughout
its whole extent in any one season. Instead, a section of the
territory within the walls is chosen for excavation each year;
the work in successive seasons is then perfectly kept in order
by the surveyor and joined together on the city plan by the
draftsmen. Thus, when the work is finished, the plans of the
city will show each successive rebuilding on the *tell* complete throughout its whole extent. In the season of 1932,
beginning as we did at the end of the Late Bronze in the section under excavation, we carried the whole section down
from Late Bronze, through Middle Bronze and Early Bronze
to rock bottom. Thus our principal work during this campaign has lain wholly in the Bronze Ages, that is to say, the
Canaanite civilization, and covered the whole Patriarchal
Period of Biblical history.

In addition to this principal work for the year, we found it
convenient, in order to keep the men always employed, and also
to connect up with our former work in 1926-28-30, to employ,
for most of the time, a smaller gang of workmen excavating
around the west gate. As in former campaigns at *Tell Beit
Mirsim,* the work at the west gate has proved to be almost
wholly in the Iron Ages, the Israelite period. Only in the gateway itself and occasionally at the very bottom of the debris,
though immediately under Early Iron I, there has been
found a very small quantity of Bronze Age material, usually
of the Early Bronze or Middle Bronze.

Now the finds begin. Besides innumerable potsherds,
usually not pretty to look at, but as important to the progress
of excavations as a calendar is to a business office, already
not a few significant articles have appeared. Hyksos scarabs,
both genuine and Palestinian imitations, are so common in
the Bronze Ages in which we are now working that they
excite little comment, but here is one genuine one of exquisite
workmanship. A finer one is never found; it is one more of
the innumerable evidences of the reign of those mysterious
people in Egypt in the Patriarchal period and of their constant,
perhaps dominant, influence in Canaan. A large and perfect

ax-head in copper or bronze testifies to the same period and to the culture of the Bronze Ages, this particular piece coming from the end of "C" level, the Late Bronze Age, and just preceding the incoming of the Israelites. A small but beautifully decorated alabaster vase comes also from the same Age, but, unfortunately, the workman's pick struck it and shattered it. Skill and glue restored its form and its evidential value, but its beauty is much marred.

In addition to these small finds are two of much greater significance. As the debris was cleared down to the floor level "D," Middle Bronze Age, it became at once apparent even to the eye of a casual observer that Kirjath-sepher has also its "Tyropeon Valley," as had Jerusalem. The section we are excavating lies directly across that small likeness of the far greater Tyropeon. Thus we shall probably find it growing deeper and deeper down to Early Bronze level at the bottom, where it goes out under the great Canaanite wall on the south side of the fortress. It does not augur well for the portion of the city to be found in this valley, for the best things are not built in the bottom of a ravine.

The most interesting of all our finds at the beginning of our work is the gruesome record of a family tragedy. In a destruction which took place about the middle of the Late Bronze Age, some time before the conquest of the city by Othniel (was it perhaps one of the incursions of the Khabiri so frequently noted in the *Tell el-Amarna* tablets?), three persons lost their lives, apparently a woman, perhaps the mother, a young lad, and a baby. They had not been buried, but the bodies were disposed in somewhat orderly fashion as though arranged thus purposely. A fallen wall covered them, but could hardly have been the immediate cause of their death, as they certainly would not arrange themselves in order for a wall to fall on them. The baby lay between the mother's limbs, as though in her helplessness it had crept there. Such are the tragedies of war always.

Another object that I photographed was a watering trough, reminiscent for us of the days of the supremacy of the horse. How like last year's bird's nest a watering trough now looks. The courtyard of this large house of "D" level, patriarchal times, gives a glimpse of daily life in the cities of Canaan while the Israelites were in Egypt. If the watering trough reveals life in the courtyard, this exquisite vase of the same period shows us into the household of some Canaanite matron. The shape of this vase has never been surpassed in ceramics, and the surface finish is equal to the shape. Yet some scholars in days gone by have thought the Canaanites in patriarchal times to be a most uncultured people. They did certainly live the simple life; people so live yet in this land. They did not, and do not, trouble themselves about being comfortable, as do especially Americans. Most of these worry more about their comfort than about either their character or their salvation. Comfort is not our Goddess of Liberty, but certainly is our goddess of thralldom.

We had almost dared to hope that in the poverty of the people we should be spared this year the rather irksome pleasure of feasts, but alas, invitations have begun. This one involves a walk of near a dozen miles or a ride of some fifty-five miles. The *mukhtar* is a wealthy man and will not, even in these profitless times, be negligent of the courtesy which custom requires toward these foreigners among his people. How hospitable this people! I passed by the poor, half-withered garden of a man on the north side of the *tell*. He introduced his three young daughters; and immediately one of them selected a very large specimen of *kusa*, a kind of cucumber, and the father presented it to me (note the hospitality of Abram and of Manoah). I was ashamed to rob their table, but must not slight his well-meant hospitality. We live well in our own dining-room, but in the poverty of the fields and gardens, most of our food must be brought from the Jerusalem market.

I wish that all who read archæological articles, and especially those who still have a lingering suspicion that the conclusions of archæologists are for the most part imagination, the imagination of "things that never were," could see what I have just been watching up on the *tell*. Our Egyptian surveyor, who for now the third season has done our surveying, or directed all who assisted in it, was working over his plane table. Deliberate, punctiliously careful, the typical mathematician, he was taking bearings, noting levels, measuring distances, directing his two young Arab assistants with the tape measure and the plummet and carefully building up the diagram of the city plan at the various levels. No one could observe the mathematical accuracy with which the work of excavation is done and the conclusions drawn without acquiring a confidence in the scientific work now being done in Bible lands. It is this that gives finality to the findings and is now turning critics more and more toward conservative interpretations, that is to say, to the interpretations attested by the surveyor and the architect and the expert in ceramics of the various ages of culture. The subjective speculations of criticism, however plausible, cannot stand for a moment against logarithms and tangents and co-tangents and the abiding forms of pottery any better than the medical practitioner of a century ago with his leeches and his lancet could hold his own among the laboratory trained men in our hospitals today. The carefully selected archæological staff of today has not only its surveyor and architect and pottery experts and draftsmen and photographers, but philologists and accomplished archæologists, and withal men who know the Bible also.

Now at the end of three weeks, we have struck our pace; trifling affairs get under way quickly, important events must acquire momentum. Important and careful work of excavation requires three weeks to clear away the rubbish, organize the work and the workers, and gain momentum. Then for four weeks things come and go with a rush, then one week is needed to close up the work and fill in again the soil for the farmer's crops. Now, I say, important finds are coming in thick and fast. Every day, nearly every hour, has its sensation. The great "E" level, the second city from the last in the Middle Bronze Age, which was poor in remains in the last season's work, is a very fine city in the section which we are now excavating. Palaces and slums are here, "Park Avenue and the Bowery"; as usual, the palaces on high ground and the hovels in the depth of the "Tyropeon Valley" of Kirjath-sepher.

But we must not forget the great house of the succeeding city, "D" level, in which was found the snake goddess in 1928 and also the set of dice in 1930. It must have been a nobleman's house in the feudal age, the late Patriarchal Period. It was, indeed, a great house of many rooms and, like a feudal castle, was surrounded by a wall fully four feet thick. The "E" level palaces were not quite so large nor so formidable in appearance, but from them have come most beautiful things. The piece of alabaster reported last week has now become a whole series of exquisite small vases in veined alabaster and of most graceful form. This collection, all from one house, indeed from a single room in that house, must have been the pride of its owner. From the same house of the Patriarchal Period about 1700 B. C., not far from the date of the descent of Jacob into Egypt, is also a remarkable collection of pottery. The one beautiful vase of the typical Middle Bronze shape already reported, has now also become a charming collection of small vases of exquisite form and finish. Continually the former conception of the Patriarchal Period as lacking in culture must be revised upward and still upward; the artistic character of these pieces has never been surpassed. It is the sublimity of simple beauty of form and finish without anything even approaching garish decoration.

Of less artistic beauty, but more utility are these two mortars with three feet, eight inches and twelve inches, respectively, in diameter. We have also the first clear indication of the character of the wooden beams in the houses from this little heap of charcoal not so completely burned but that it shows unmistakably the grain of oak wood. Occasionally curious and surprising things appear, as along with things of great beauty (level "D"), strainers shaped exactly like the candlesticks we knew in our childhood and which sometimes are still given one in the bedrooms of European hotels. The saucer shape is the same and the round ring for a finger hold, but instead of the candlestick rising above, there is a strainer below. Unfortunately every one yet found has the strainer broken off, but several of the strainers themselves have been found.

The fourth week of excavation this season starts off well. The great "D" level in which was found the snake goddess is being carried down now toward the mountain-top. A number of interesting things have come to light. The most important is a perfect specimen of bronze mold for making weapons and tools. Other molds in broken and imperfect state have been found, one is in the Bible Lands Museum of Pittsburgh-Xenia Seminary; but this is a large one with molds on three sides and unbroken. On one side is a mold for a great curved sword, not a scimitar, but more the shape of a machete, only slightly curved. On other parts of the mold are places for axes or adzes, and for spear and pike. The mold is blackened from the touch of the hot metal.

The constant appearance of Hyksos scarabs, both genuine and imitation, continues to heap up the already overwhelming evidence that the Patriarchal Period and Hyksos times were contemporaneous. Most of these scarabs are of quite conventional decorations, but one is a royal scarab; it reads, *Yqb* or *Ykb* ("lord of two lands giving life forever"). This is most suggestive of the well-known Jacob scarabs, but. is spelled differently and may possibly not be intended for the same name, though probability is in its favor. Jacob in Hebrew is spelled *Ya'qob*. In the Jacob scarabs, well-known, the name is spelled with the strong Egyptian vowel letter "a," and there is added to the name the Egyptian form of the Hebrew divine name *El* after the fashion of Egyptian royal names which added to the personal name also a divine name. In this scarab the spelling is different. The "y" is distinct, but the vowel letter "a" is wanting, and no divine name is appended, though divine attributes are asserted, "giving life." It seems to be an imitation scarab and was probably made by one who did not know how to spell Hebrew names in Egyptian hieroglyphs; but of that we cannot be sure; it may be an entirely different name. We need always to keep humbly in mind that even a poor scribe knew better how to write hieroglyphs than most Egyptologists (perhaps all) know how to read them!

Concerning Jacob scarabs, much caution is needed. It is so easy to slip from the identity of sound to the identity of persons. There is no evidence that the Jacob of the scarabs was the Jacob of the Bible narrative. Indeed, it is quite certain that they were not the same person. Certainly there is no intimation in the Bible that Jacob became a Pharaoh of Egypt. The evidence of these Jacob scarabs is of a different kind; the name is unmistakably a Hebrew name and implies that either the Hyksos were Semites among whose royal persons a Jacob might be found, or that the Israelites, who certainly were in great favor with the Hyksos, may have come to such place and importance, as we know Joseph did, that some of their number ultimately came to the throne. In any case, the finding of this *Yqb* scarab adds another chapter to the consideration of the subject.

At least three different forms of the inscription on "Jacob" scarabs are known. Some Egyptologists think that they represent different Jacobs. It is quite possible, however, that they only represent different scribes, for Egyptian scribes are always put to their wits end to know how to represent Semitic names in Egyptian characters. Two or three of the scarabs have the name represented with many hieroglyphs, as one found by Petrie, and one by Sethe. Another found by Muller was written in much shorter form. Our "Jacob" scarab this year, found at *Tell Beit Mirsim*, is the shortest of all the forms, having only *Yqb* (as they omitted vowels). This scarab will take its place along with the others that have been found with the hope that some day we shall know the history represented by the "Jacob" scarabs.

Bronzes occur very frequently in this Middle Bronze Age, as a matter of course; *iron not at all*. Most of the bronzes now coming out are not large, but, on the other hand, quite delicate; this tiny chisel so perfectly made — one can only wonder for what purpose it was intended. Bronze needles of this land are usually large for coarse leather work, and these are no exception. Here, however, is one large ax-head apparently for carpentry, to be set in a wooden handle and used as an adze.

This "E" level, together with the "D" level preceding it as we go down, is now about cleared; the workmen are today carrying away all the rubbish to give a clear field for the surveyor and the photographer; and then we shall go down to the "F" and "G" levels and uncover the whole of the Abrahamic house of which we found the court in 1930, and walk again in Abrahamic surroundings.

"How thrilling! You must live all the time in a fever of expectation." Such was the enthusiastic exclamation of a lady who recently visited our work. Do we live in a roseate world? We do not! Often only the urge to do our duty under whatever difficulties keeps us diligent. There are days when nothing comes out, at least nothing but dust. The heat of the sun hour after hour drives us all to shelter. Sometimes when the sky is clear and the sun bright, in fact the day most

beautiful, there is a quality in the air that threatens to pros-
trate us all; the workmen drag their feet, even the Egyptian
foremen, who can stand any heat that assails human kind,
are languid. It was so yesterday, and this morning a south
wind blows, not precisely the "east wind" to which the Bible
gives such a bad name, but it is at least a near relative of it,
and probably explains our languor of yesterday. Then sometimes sand-flies disturb our sleep, and a heavy dew drifts into
the tent to dampen the bedding and chill our feet before
morning. As a result of all these harassing trifles hardly a
day goes by that some one's appetite does not need to be
pampered, and today the old *Khawadjah* is going up to Jerusalem to keep out of the sun until his appetite returns. Is all
this to the debit side of our account? Not at all; without
these experiences we should not know the land of the Book,
and only when we know it, do we know the Book. Not one
of us would exchange his place and his opportunity for the
softest berth in the homeland. Besides, the evenings are
delightful beyond what any summer resort in the homeland
can supply, and we have always the consciousness that we are
in the front-line trenches of the battle of religions. The day
of mere opinions has gone by; the facts are demanded, and
we are daily digging them up.

Now again to the record of those facts. A man who had a
family quarrel in which he tried to embroil us had left the
work, but after some days returned, and the first day of his
work he turned over a couple of beads for which he was given
a half piaster bakhsheesh. When Dr. Kelso had brought them
in and cleaned them of the dust clinging to them, he found
them beautiful, ribbed gold beads. In all our work we have
never before found any trace of gold except the few tiny
pieces of gold leaf. Indeed, we are not anxious to find gold,
as it is likely to make the workmen avaricious and tempt
them to dishonesty. But we try to reward them for faithfulness, so Dr. Kelso went back to the *tell* and gave the man
five piasters bonus for each bead. Thus his first day on the
work again netted him in bakhsheesh more than his day's
wages. The wisdom of this method has been questioned,
even combated by some, but the workmen seem to have in a
sense a claim; to them it seems that these things belong to
the neighborhood and that they should have some share in

the finds. At least, it seems fair to give them a share and, if the method is not abused, it works well. Trifling as two beads seem, they are an indication of the refinements of life of the age to which they belong, one more touch to the picture of Patriarchal culture. When associated, as they are here, with ivory inlay from furniture, they indicate much for the beauty of the homes, which from the size of them were truly palatial.

Another touch of refinement is of a slightly different char- acter, a badly burned piece of Egyptian faience in the form of a small pilgrim bottle. These flasks, really small canteens, were introduced about the beginning of the Late Bronze Age. This was a time of the great popularity of imported things, imported usually from Cyprus and the Greek islands. Nearly all the pottery of that age was either imported or an imi- tation of imported ware. Occasionally a piece of Egyptian faience appears, and this piece was such. It is an unsightly object in its burned condition, but sufficient traces of the beauty of it remained so that our architect, Mr. Detweiler, was able to reconstruct the whole pattern. It was most artis- tic, and, when in the resplendent colors of the faience, must have been an object of great beauty. Another touch of the artistic is seen in two pieces of ivory inlay of furniture on which are drawn, with much life and vigor, two gazelles.

Now I must go up to the *tell* and take a motion picture of the progress of the work as we go down to examine that Abrahamic house uncovered in part in 1930. It belonged to the feudal age of which we have this year been seeing much in the palaces and walled castles of the feudal barons of that Hyksos age in this land. The great mystery in both Egypt and Palestine is the Hyksos mystery. The regular stratifi- cation of this mound at *Tell Beit Mirsim* gives hope that at some time in the course of our excavations here that mystery may be cleared up. Or perhaps any day some inscription may be found which will throw light upon the history of that Sphinx-like people.

Certainly it is the unexpected that happens. I came down from Jerusalem this morning hoping for something great, I knew not what. Soon after lunch there was brought in from the *tell* the most beautiful seal cylinder yet found in Pales-

tine. The Egyptian scholars and the Babylonian scholars on
the staff are busy puzzling over the strange concatenation
of characters which usually go into the make-up of a seal
cylinder. Many things are not yet clear concerning the inscription on this cylinder, but some things are clear enough.
It was cut by a sculptor who was a consummate artist. The
stronger the magnifying glass we put on it, and the more we
enlarge a photograph of it, the more perfect the work of the
artist seems to be. Now this beautiful work is unmistakably
identified as between 1700 and 1600 B. C., a little after the
time of Abraham. This identification is made both by the
stratification in the mound and the pottery surrounding the
seal which is certainly of that age. Then the archæology
of the inscription as compared with other seal cylinders points
to the same time.

The symbolical character of the seal is quite as interesting
and puzzling as the skill of the engraver. It is certainly a
combination of Egyptian and Babylonian symbolism and inscriptions, and there are some enigmatic marks upon it which
suggest that there may possibly be a third script. All this is in
keeping with the well-known mixture of cultures in the Hyksos
age. There are two principal characters on the seal; one, on
the right, is Egyptian with the name in Egyptian hierglyphs.
Opposite to him is a Babylonian character, the god Nabu,
whose name in cuneiform characters is also given, beside some
symbolical characters, birds and animals both Egyptian and
Babylonian. There is one column of Egyptian hieroglyphs
clearly cut and perfectly legible, the interpretation of which is
very puzzling. The phonetic equivalent of the hieroglyphs is
simply *Yhst.*

In addition to this seal cylinder were several inferior ones,
one of them of fairly good quality, a copy of the so-called
"tree of Paradise," two figures under a fruit tree. The serpent was wanting under this tree. There was also found in
the "E" level a remarkable griffin scarab. It had the head
of a bird, a rather grotesque head, the body and tail of a lion,
and the wings of a great bird. The symbolism of the griffin
is not well understood. It is easy to give fanciful interpretations to it. On the other hand it is certain that to the
ancients, the grotesque combination of the characteristics of

various animals in one symbol had very definite meaning. If fully understood now, not only would the symbolism of mythology be intelligible, but the striking illustrations of an Ezekiel, or even of a John in the Apocalypse, would become clear to us. That both Ezekiel and John did understand the symbolism cannot be doubted. The varied interpretations given to their symbolism by the commentators indicate that few, if any, commentators understand the symbolism now. The folly of building up theological systems, or parts of theological systems, upon such uncertain interpretation, is very apparent. But with the discovery of these griffins in different ages we are learning the history of the development of art and symbolism, and some time symbolism, including that of Ezekiel and John, will be understood.

The great value of our discoveries in this Middle Bronze Age, in the very best period of it, at the height of Canaanite culture, the culture of patriarchal times, and which is indeed also the climax of our study of the history of culture in Palestine, is that the character of the culture of those times is now definitely determined. The attitude of criticism for many decades has been that of extreme skepticism toward any degree of culture in the patriarchal age. The whole historical interpretation of the literature of Israel rests upon this assumption. Now the superior quality of the ceramics and the engraving and other works of art of this period, not forgetting the ivory inlay of furniture described in the campaign of 1930, shows beyond any reasonable doubt that the patriarchal period was one of a high degree of culture, the highest culture indeed in this land before Greek and Roman times. If it be urged that the discoveries are comparatively few in number and indicate definitely only certain forms of development, it may be recalled to mind that culture, like leaven, spreads in every direction.

Undoubtedly their ideas of culture were very different from ours. Personal and individual comfort is the twentieth century idea of culture, and beauty for its own sake has no great representatives at the present time, either in painting, or in music, or in poetry. The ancients, like their modern descendants in this land, were not seriously troubled in mind about personal comfort, but attached the highest importance, on the one hand, to the necessities of life including protection and, on the other hand, to things of beauty for beauty's own sake.

For several days interest has been intense and excitement great. The workmen found a rock-cut tunnel. Now people do not cut their way through solid rock without a purpose in view and presumably an adequate purpose. It might be that they were on their way to a secret water supply, a spring deep in earth, as at Gezer and now at Megiddo. Or it might be that a rock-cut tomb was being projected to which this was the approach. Or still again a secret hiding place for an archive or other treasure, which needed to be safely preserved.

The approaching tunnel was narrow and steep and in places quite low, and so a difficult way. For this reason, the idea of a spring was speedily ruled out; the approach to a spring must manifestly be as easy as possible. At Gezer one might drive down in a coach and four, at Megiddo a great shaft with a staircase was the entrance. Evidently this was a place to which approach would not be frequent, hence a tomb or an archive. The workmen dug on, the course of the tunnel changed and it sank deeper and deeper into the ground, and then, suddenly, a jamb appeared on the right and the left and a room opened out before them. All had been filled up with soil carried in or sifted in through cracks. So it was with feverish work that we cleared out the little room, hoping that it was but the ante-chamber to some important hiding place. Visions of a rich tomb or an old library or rich treasure of a king flitted before our imagination.

Alas! The room was empty, there seemed nothing beyond it. It is ever so with the excavator; it is the unexpected that happens, and worse still, the expected does not happen. We go right on with our work and tomorrow we may make the great discovery, wholly unexpected.

A Glimpse at the Pottery Yard

Before me as I write is the pottery yard, the large open space of the former threshing-floor, in which are the hundreds of baskets of pottery, each carefully marked that we may know whence it came; and there in the hot sun (the thermometer now stands at 101) the brushers work cleaning the pottery from the lime that clings to it; and there also are the Director, Dr. Albright, and his assistant, Dr. Kelso, carefully examining the heaps that have been brushed, and near by our Egyptian pottery expert who matches the fragments and puts together the valuable pieces. Now and again some one comes in with a group of pots thus put together, which, then, the draftsmen at the table where I write, carefully draw. Thus the work goes on and the results accumulate that show so conclusively the trustworthiness of the Biblical narratives as we have them.

This theme just announced need not cause surprise by its frequent recurrence. The work here at *Tell Beit Mirsim* has added, year by year, to the accumulated facts until they are becoming absolutely overwhelming. Dr. Garstang, in his address before the Victoria Institute, and again in his recent work on Palestinian archæology and the books of Joshua-Judges showed so conclusively that the archæological remains of the civilization of the time of the Judges agreed most exactly with the narrative as it now stands, and not at all with the reconstructed narrative as arranged by many critics. Now what he showed so satisfactorily for the period of the Judges, the work here at old Kirjath-sepher this year has shown even more conclusively for the record of the period of the Patriarchs. The facts harmonize exactly with the requirements, literary, moral, and religious, of the narratives as they stand in the Biblical record, and do not agree with such records reconstructed and brought down to a late date.

The pottery, superior in shape and finish, presenting the most cherished designs for bric-a-brac today; the beautiful grained alabastrons for decorative use; and especially the practical perfection of the art of engraving as exemplified in the seal cylinder; together with the rich ivory inlay of furniture reveal an artistic development of civilization and culture entirely in keeping with the requirements of the narrative, and in particulars going far beyond anything the expectation of which would be aroused by a study of the Biblical account. The Patriarchal Age, in fact, was indeed a time of culture of a higher order in material things than ever afterwards attained in this land until Greek and Roman times.

Again the cave; it was difficult to conclude that the promising prospect was merely a dry hole. So the diggers still dug on, and again visions of a second room and perhaps a royal tomb or a secreted treasure lured us. But alas, again! the *Reis,* our competent Egyptian foreman, called the men out of the tunnel; there was danger of a cave-in from above and he would not endanger the men. The surveyor confirmed the order and so, we shall complete the excavation of the section of the *tell* upon which we are engaged and then, if there be time yet this campaign, we shall try to sink a shaft to reach the tunnel. If we have not time for this now, it must await another campaign.

A House of Abraham's Time

We may recall to mind the "Abrahamic house" which we discovered in the 1930 campaign, the house which reflected exactly the sociological and political conditions implied in the story of Lot and the angels. There was the great strong wall with the big door socket *in situ* indicating just such a door as could resist a mob as did the door in Lot's house. We have now come down to the "G" level at that point in the excavations and have been uncovering the house of which that great door socket represented the entrance to the court. The rooms back of the great court are small and give evidence of a terrific conflagration. The floor of the first room is deeply covered with ashes, black ashes and charcoal. The men have been sifting them in hope of recovering some treasured article, but so far all seems to have perished in the great fire that destroyed the city. It is especially indicative, however, that this house seems to have been the center of the fire; probably it was as important as that of Lot at Sodom, the house of a rich man, one of the feudal barons of that beginning of the feudal Age in Palestinian history; a social state of the country which continued all through the Patriarchal age. Probably Lot came to be in Sodom what these feudal barons were all over Palestine throughout the Hyksos period.

Just now comes in one of those beautiful faience flasks, once beautiful, but now so destroyed in its decoration that its beauty of coloring is all gone; only something of the design that can be projected by our artist, and the shape of the tiny flask in all its delicate outline still remains. Do you wonder that we are forced to the conclusion that there was

a high culture in Patriarchal days, despite the fact that
there is such a dilapidated condition of the ruins? The
ruins of a burned house present much the same confusion
after thirty years as of the three thousand years these ruins
have lain here.

Today we had visitors, archeological visitors. We are
always glad to have such; they are intensely interested and
usually have a clear comprehension of the meaning of
things. It makes all the difference in the world, when you
talk on a subject, whether your audience understands anything or not. These people understood. Dr. Glueck, Director of the American School in Jerusalem, who is *ex-officio*
a member of our staff and has been here most of the season,
brought down today most of the members of the summer
school. They consist almost entirely of the company or-
ganized by Dr. Jackson of the Methodist American University, Washington, who for some time has been bringing out a
class every year to the American School. Two years ago
there were nearly forty in the class, this year only a little
over twenty. Most of them are ministers of the Gospel,
others, especially the ladies, are teachers in various Bible
schools or are special Bible students. We devoted ourselves
for the hour and a half that they stayed to showing them
the work on the *tell* and as many as possible of the interesting finds already described. The finds always interest
visitors very much. At the excavations themselves they
look on with a decided air of puzzlement. The old idea that
there is "a lot of imagination about it" is very widespread
and persistent. Most of them, if we did not show them the
individual objects found and explain the meaning of them,
would go away with a rather persistent impression that the
whole work was a humbug. On the other hand, I think that
on this occasion we made very deep the impression that I
am trying to convey, that of the remarkable evidence we
are getting of a high state of culture in the Patriarchal
times. Tomorrow we expect two of the archeological specialists, Père Vincent of the *École Saint Étienne,* Jerusalem,
and Mr. Alan Rowe, who did much of the work at Beisan.
These men will help us more than we help them.

The experiences of a day in camp at this old *tell* have
the varied imagery of the Homeric poems and all the morn-

ing and evening glory of Ruben's sunrises and sunsets. Then
we have now in the middle of August all the varied experiences of temperature from crawling out from under double
blankets at four-thirty in the morning to sweltering in sun-
hat and under an umbrella on the *tell* at noonday, and
again sitting in evening enjoyment of a delightful sea-
breeze unsurpassed at Biarritz, Scheveningen, or Atlantic
City in the glory of the season. Then from marveling at the
saffron and gold afterglow of sunset we seek our couches
for the refreshing sleep of childhood. Somewhere in the
record of these campaigns I have said that Palestine has all
the varieties of climate and has them all the time. We are
now experiencing this day by day. The only exception is
that as this is the dry season our experiences are never
varied by rainfall. This marvelous variety of daily experience it is that makes the special adaptability of this
land to be the homeland of a world revelation. From
Greenland's icy mountains to India's coral strand, the Book
records human experiences. No other small land in all the
world would have been able to portray so universally
human experiences and human emotions. For a like reason
it was appropriate that the Son of Man should be a man of
Galilee. He was near to our human nature to reveal God,
and a man of Palestine that he might be near to all of us.

Those who know only the small blue or green grapes of
eastern America or the wine and raisin grapes of the Pacific
coast have little conception of the grapes of Palestine. We
are reveling in their lusciousness at the table these days at
Tell Beit Mirsim. And as we go to Jerusalem and back,
passing as we do the most wonderful grape region, that of
the Hebron district, the Plain of Mamre and the terraced
hills round about, the deep green of the vines not trained
up on trellises generally, but sprawling upon the dry
ground, is a continual delight to the eyes so filled these hot
summer days with the yellow, bare fields and gray mountain sides. In these vineyards, as in so many other things,
we are constantly introduced to the facts of this land so remarkably delineated in the Bible narrative. Not a few
people stumble over the grape cluster tale of the spies as
an exaggeration, of a piece with the fear-inspired report of
cities "walled up to heaven." And now the doubters of the

grape story might have had their eyes opened as our cook brought to the table at lunch time today one cluster of grapes that weighed more than five pounds!

The work of which we write is also cosmopolitan; for the book is a world Book, the land is in a sense a world land which illustrates, as we have noted, all elevations and all climates, if not at all times, at least at most unexpected times. The revelation was to be cosmopolitan and it was given a cosmopolitan setting. It may seem that these remarks are apropos of nothing. Not so. We of the staff of the expedition at *Tell Beit Mirsim* in 1932 are also cosmopolitan. A few days ago when some members of the staff were on an exploring expedition, four remaining members sat down to lunch together. One of them, Dr. Albright, was born on the South American continent; another, Dr. Kelso, was born on the North American continent; a third, Dr. Schmidt, was born on the European continent. The fourth member, Mr. William Gad, was born on the African continent, and all of these together sat down to the table in Asia. Surely we may claim to fit in quite well with the cosmopolitan character of the Bible.

Sadness has fallen upon the camp. Day before yesterday I came down from Jerusalem with some friends who went back in the evening around by Gaza and *Bab el-Wad*. Yesterday a car came down from Jerusalem, sent by Mrs. Kyle, with the dreadful announcement that Mr. Jacob Spafford, of the American Colony, so well known to many Palestine travelers, had been killed in an automobile accident in going over the mountain range about five miles from Jerusalem. For now almost exactly forty years the Colony has been my Jerusalem home, and in all that time, Mr. Spafford has been an intimate and valued friend. He was a devout Christian gentleman, though born a Jew. His funeral was attended by a very large and cosmopolitan company of friends— Americans, Englishmen, Swedes, Arabs, Jews, Protestants, and Roman Catholics. My life is deeply saddened. But there is one special comfort as so many of our friends on earth are taken home to Heaven; we come to have more friends awaiting us over there than will be left to mourn us here.

We have now in the main section of our excavations got-

ten down to the Age just preceding Abraham, "H"-"I" levels
and the Early Bronze "J" level, the most ancient city on the
mountain top, and some surprising things are coming out.
During most of this year large pots have been singularly
scarce, but now from this earliest occupation but one on the
mountain we are getting a mixture of Early Bronze and
Middle Bronze, for this we found in 1930 to be a transition
period. Usually the pottery of this time and particularly
the Early Bronze types have been of coarse texture and
ofttimes crudely made. But here we have some fine, smooth
pots of the finest texture in clay and well made on the
wheel. One very large pot of Early Bronze type, with the
distinctive flat bottom, is of fine whitish clay, thin in the
walls, of clay of very fine texture, and of unusual and most
shapely form. It is but slightly decorated with a few parallel
rings around the pot near the top. Much of the Early Bronze
pottery, that preceding Abraham's time, while strong and
useful, was inferior in texture and workmanship; but it is
apparent that there were fine things produced in that age
also. And the degree of culture of any age must be estimated from the best it could turn out. Thus much the same
high state of culture which we have seen in the Patriarchal
age must be predicated also of the time immediately preceding Abraham.

It is true that a nation could not live its life on such
artistic trinkets as these of the Patriarchal Period, but does
anyone suppose for a moment that they did so; can anyone
believe that a people who produced such things as these,
these trinkets that we are also to find now, produced nothing
for themselves that contributed to utility and comfort? A
utilitarian age may exist without a high state of artistic
culture. We have a rather bad example of such a mechanical
civilization today; we boast of mass production, but poets
and painters and musicians are not produced that way. On
the other hand, a culture that produces high art finds some
way to meet the demands for comfort and utility. Abstractly
stated, culture tends to meet the whole demand of life in the
situation in which it may be placed.

So not the quantity, but the quality, of these discoveries
during the past year attests a culture for Patriarchal times
surely as high as anything demanded by the Patriarchal

narrative. This is what Dr. Garstang, by his researches, showed for the age of the books of Joshua and Judges (a conclusion which I had reached and published in 1912 in *The Deciding Voice of the Monuments,* p. 260, first edition) —that those narratives are in exact accord with the archæological conditions which prevailed and that those conditions do not accord with the reconstructed narrative of criticism. Now the climax of our investigation here this season shows that what was true of the early age of Israelite history was true also of this earlier age of Canaanite history.

A recent writer on New Testament problems puts forth this dictum, that it is never safe to tie up our faith in a religion to the historical narratives with which the religion is associated; because historical narratives are subject to scientific testing and to historical research. The archæologist in Bible Lands has no such fear. Whether he be Christian or Jew, he recognizes that his religion is a historical religion and he welcomes scientific testing and historical research in firm reliance upon the very different dictum, that the Culture of Bible Lands is the Matrix of Bible Narratives; if the religion is true, the narratives must fit and he uniformly finds that they do fit.

The archæological discoveries exactly accord with the demand of the Biblical narrative of culture in each period.

COMPARATIVE VIEW OF TYPES OF POTTERY

Fig. 1, Early Bronze   Fig. 2, Middle Bronze
Fig. 3, Late Bronze   Fig. 4, Early Iron I
Fig 5, Early Iron II   Fig. 6. Early Iron III
Only the Post-Exilic Pottery (Fig. 6) is lacking at
Tell Beit Mirsim
(Text on page 191)

PLATE XVI

CHAPTER X

THE SUMMARY OF RESULTS

Camp *Tell Beit Mirsim.*

AT Camp *Tell Beit Mirsim* we have two tents in which are gathered together and piled up on tables hundreds of things discovered and entered in our big record book. They are all there and any one of our visitors or readers might see them there; but very few, having looked upon them, would have any very definite idea of what we had done with all this expenditure of time and money. It is one thing to *see* things and it is oftentimes quite another thing to *see what they mean.*

From week to week, even from day to day, I have kept the readers informed in order of the discoveries made; but it is not very much easier to know clearly what all these things mean from having read about them than from having seen them at the tent. Most of those who would visit us at the camp would still say, "Now what do all these things mean? Of what value are they?" Or perhaps they might say as a gentleman said to me recently, "What do all these things contribute to spiritual life?"

I will make my reply now as I made it then to him. The spiritual life, piety, is the ultimate aim; but our piety rests upon a foundation of faith in the Word of God. There are a great many people in the world of this day who are exerting themselves to discredit the Bible. The work of the archæologist is the only work today that gets the facts, and the facts are attesting the trustworthiness of the Bible. So when anyone asks, "What does your work do for piety?" I reply, "If the foundations be destroyed, what can the righteous do?" Piety would be left suspended in the air. So the most important questions concerning our work are, "What came out of Kirjath-sepher in 1926-1932? What evidence has appeared to attest the foundations?" A little time will be devoted to the answering of these questions. First we shall see the history of civilization in Palestine as

189

revealed especially here at Kirjath-sepher, and then consider a long series of historical parallels between the Biblical narratives and the history of culture that we have discovered.

To one who stands and looks at the great fortress here on this hill it is difficult to realize that this city which goes so far back in antiquity had a very definite beginning: *there was a time when there was no city here.* And we know about that time. To most Bible readers Abram at his call from Chaldea seems to mark the starting point of history in this land. But long before Abram responded to God's call in Chaldea the beginnings of a city, at least a village, stood here on this mountain top. The Canaanite came here to this height of delightful sea breezes and pitched his sprawling black tent amid the stones on the mountain top. There were no houses here as yet and, of course, no wall was built. This mountain top with its great boulders was used unimproved exactly as we have found it at the bottom of the debris.

Now, as we leave the Early Bronze Age and come up to the Middle Bronze Age, we enter what was probably a period of many civil wars. There was but one city built and destroyed in the Early Bronze Age. In the Middle Bronze there were in all four cities. Below these Middle Bronze cities and immediately above the city of the Early Bronze are two cities in which there is the mixture of pottery, the transitional period. Evidently the Middle Bronze Age did not come in with a catastrophe, but by gradual infiltration, not a "peaceful penetration," for again and again the city was burned. But as there was no sudden change in the pottery, so no new civilization coming in, but civil strife. Most of the distinctively Early Bronze shapes still appear, the ledge handles, the inverted rims, and the great coarse ware; but with these there is also the beautiful thin pottery and the prow-shaped bowls and other Middle Bronze characteristics. This is exactly as at the Moabite temple at Ader, found in 1924, which represented the age immediately succeeding the destruction of the Cities of the Plain. It is a fascinating work of investigation to note how exactly the cultural remains of these places attest each other and corroborate the Biblical record.

Next above these two cities of the transition period, in the Middle Bronze Age, and now exclusively Middle Bronze without mixture of Early Bronze, are four more cities each succeeding its predecessor above a level of ashes and lime and blackened debris, gruesome reminders of the turmoil of those times of civil strife. I say civil strife, for strife terrific there certainly was which left a trail of blood and ashes, yet there is no indication of any change in civilization. There is in all these four cities the same black juglets of the Hyksos pottery, and the same carinated, prow-shaped bowls of beautiful thin ware, and everywhere and always the evidence of an age of turmoil. It is always so throughout the East in that age. Who and what and whence these Hyksos? Why was their hand against every man around them, and why favorable to the Israelites so as to give them asylum and long years of prosperity under royal patronage in Egypt? It was in this age, it will be recalled, that was noted also the identity of the pottery with that found in Cyprus and among the Hittites and even in the Greek remains from the region of Troy. Were the Hyksos ancient Scythians or an earlier Tamerlane or some unknown devastating horde out of the north, whence, in all ages, ravishers of civilization have been wont to come periodically? I repeat, if we could find whence *came this beautiful pottery and the clay of which it was made,* we might answer these questions.

Next above the Middle Bronze city was the city of the Late Bronze Age. Here again there was strife and in part, at least, the city was destroyed, really giving two cities to this Late Bronze Age. The age came in by dreadful catastrophe. Violence must have been rampant, for there was not immediate occupation. Only slowly does the pottery of the Late Bronze Age appear. When it does appear, there are, indeed, strange shapes. People sometimes wonder how we can distinguish the ages. If only they could see a collection of pottery of the various ages arranged in order, they would not wonder; the differences between the Middle and Late Bronze are so striking as to appear at a glance. Instead of the delicate shapes and fine, thin ware of the Middle Bronze, here we have painted pots from Greek lands, Mycenæan ware, and peculiar, staggering Cypro-

Phœnician wine jugs and smaller vases of similar shape for perfumes. The lamps also now began to have the closely pinched lip so familiar in later ages. Not much was learned of the religion of these Canaanites other than the serpent worship learned of in 1928 from the idol found then. Now, however, we find the lioness and the small offering table for the pouring of libations. It is a curious, rather grotesque object, as I have described it in the account from week to week. Whether or not the lion decoration is merely decorative in intent or has a religious significance, is not certain. There was a Babylonian deity whose symbol was the lion found in the great sculpture at Beisan. The motif of the artist in this offering table is Egyptian.

The one discovery in this part of the debris that gives some light upon Biblical history is the beautiful scarab, royal scarab, of Amenophis III. This scarab, plainly a seal-ring scarab, used by an Egyptian official at Kirjath-sepher in the reign of Amenophis III, is almost conclusive material evidence that Egypt was still in power here and that the Israelites were not yet in possession of the land. Thus this scarab has an important bearing on the date of the Exodus. The opinion strongly urged by some that, in the reign of Amenophis III, Israel was already in Palestine or at least the Exodus had already taken place, would be thus wholly inconsistent with the presence of this scarab at Kirjath-sepher at that time. While other evidence, as the great burned layer at the end of the Late Bronze, above which all is Israelite, is more positively decisive than this scarab, yet this is contributory to the same date for the Exodus and Conquest.

At the end of this Late Bronze Age we come to that greatest burning in all the history of Kirjath-sepher, the burning by Othniel at the great siege of this fortress at the time of the Conquest. The record of this event is so briefly and simply told in the books of Joshua and Judges that the sight of what was actually done comes as a revelation of the simplicity of the historical methods of the Bible. The difference between the Word and mere human history is still more apparent, when this account is compared with the boastful accounts of Egyptian and Assyrian kings concerning their wars of conquest, or even the account of the Jewish wars by Josephus. In fact, the unique method of revelation nowhere more clearly appears than in just this escape from the usual bombast of mere worldly history. What appalling and disgraceful illustrations of this difference did the Great War furnish. Only now are the various nations on both sides beginning to realize the falseness of national propaganda to excite the war spirit.

Here it was in the city built by Othniel, in the Early Iron Age I, that the "sea peoples" of whom the Egyptian historians tell us, became manifest in the history of Israel. These incomers from the islands of the sea and from the adjacent Greek lands, first settling in the north, naturally drifted southward following the course of least resistance, as race movements always do, and finding here a warmer clime and more fertile soil and so an easier life, came at last to rest north of the Sinai desert and became known to history as the Philistines. Having given their name to the land, Palestine, they gave their crafts to the Israelites and later faded away from the world's consciousness. They still live among the peasant population of this land, and in that branch of the Jewish race which still exhibits the characteristic Philistine features. The Jews did not drive them out, but mingled and inter-married with them.

The city of Othniel was destroyed by Shishak after the division of the Monarchy. The great burning that he left is second only to that made by Othniel. This city destroyed at last by Nebuchadnezzar is the best preserved of all the ten cities on this mountain. What a commentary on ruthlessness this fact is, when Nebuchadnezzar, regarded now as one of the most terrible of devastators, yet made a less terrible destruction than any of the Canaanite conquerors here or even than the Jews themselves at their entrance into the land.

Thus layer after layer we have come up through the debris of this old fortress, and down through the ages of history to the final destruction of Kirjath-sepher. We have not yet finished our study. What has come out of Kirjath-sepher? We have, in fact, only gathered together the materials and taken a look through from beginning to end that, in the next sections we may lay the materials obtained side by side with Biblical history and see what really did come out of Kirjath-sepher.

KIRJATH-SEPHER'S CONTRIBUTION TO HISTORY

How now do the events of the Biblical narratives fit into history? There is a widespread notion that a chronological scheme is not only important to history, but absolutely essential. This is flatly asserted by some chronologists and tacitly assumed by most critical scholars. Radicals make use of it to discredit the historical trustworthiness of Scripture, while others pin their faith in the Book not to its content, but to somebody's estimated chronological scheme.

In contrast with this overestimate of chronology is set the evidential value of *historical parallels,* the testing of one historical record by another of independent origin. In fact, the really supreme test of history is not a chronological scheme, but historical parallels. Chronological schemes are of mathematical character; mathematics finds expression by figures; figures are peculiarly liable to scribal and typographical errors; and, besides, figurers, being human and sometimes full of all subtlety, will manipulate figures. On the other hand, events tell the truth, they are beyond the reach of collusion; and independent records of events, especially material remains of events, and manners and customs have an evidential value greater than that supplied by any other source. Especially is this true of parallels between written records and material remains; *only real events leave anything to be dug up out of the ground.* Here thus emerges the whole argument furnished by archæological discovery.

The real results that came out at Kirjath-sepher or by comparisons with discoveries elsewhere, are thus a long series of Historical Parallels.

HISTORICAL PARALLELS

A recounting of the historical parallels, which have been sufficiently brought forward in our work and co-ordinated with others in the same field, the result of much work by many others, will be a fitting close for this review of the campaigns at *Tell Beit Mirsim.* Some reiteration of facts already presented in detail in the study of the materials will be as unobjectionable as it is inevitable in thus considering the value of what has been found.

PARALLEL 1.—*The Destruction of the Cities of the Plain and the "Great Break" in the Civilization of the Jordan Valley.* The Biblical account of the destruction of Sodom and Gomorrah and allied cities consists almost entirely of the divine elements; the people knew what had taken place, they only needed to be told what special part God had in the catastrophe. It is seldom to be expected that we should find any attestation of the divine element in miracle in historical events. But this miracle was embodied in natural events; it had some natural elements. Natural events are apt to leave material evidence which may often be discovered, and so historical events parallel to the natural elements in the miracle are often to be found.

The pottery from the graves at *Bab ed-Dra*, the great High Place of the Cities of the Plain, is the characteristic pottery of the Early Bronze Age—the rough ledge handles, the crimped ledge handles, the inverted rims and the coarse, heavy ware. Now the civilization of the Jordan Valley has been most carefully traced by Albright, Fisher, Garstang, and Père Vincent. Practically every known city in the valley has told us when it began and when, if ever, it ended. Hazor began in the Early Bronze and ended at the Early Iron I, as is related in the Book of Joshua where it is said that Joshua completely destroyed the fortress. Other cities down the valley are equally well traced in their history. Jericho began very early and, in some form at some location, has ever since continued. So the Plain was inhabited in the Early Bronze Age, but a "great break" came at the end of that age. Something happened which put an end to civilization of any sort in that region, and not again until after the end of Biblical history did this region have any history except a history of ruins mentioned in the classics. Now the cultural remains show exactly the same. For twenty-five hundred years after that "great break" no kind of civilization was on the Plain. Thus the history dug up parallels and attests the Biblical narrative.

PARALLEL 2.—*The "Great Break"—and the Early Bronze Age at Kirjath-sepher.* In that earliest city in the great fortress at *Tell Beit Mirsim* were exactly the same forms of Early Bronze pottery as those found at *Bab ed-Dra* at the remains of the great High Place of the Cities of the Plain.

So exactly were the potsherds alike that they might be exchanged in the characteristic types and it would not be possible to separate them except by knowing the origin of each piece. Thus the beginning of the city of Kirjath-sepher was contemporaneous with the great catastrophe on the Plain. Nothing is yet indicated concerning the date of these parallel events, but of that later.

PARALLEL 3.—*The Early Bronze Age at Kirjath-sepher— and at Gezer, and the Twelfth and Early Thirteenth Dynasties in Egypt.* Macalister in his long and epoch making work at Gezer found in what he calls the First Semitic Age, now called Early Bronze, again the same types as at *Bab ed-Dra* and at Kirjath-sepher. So exactly are the types of pottery alike that there can be no doubt that they all represent the same period of history. But in the same layer of debris in which he found this pottery he found Egyptian remains and among them the scarabs of the Twelfth and Early Thirteenth Dynasties. These can now be quite accurately dated as of the early part of the nineteenth century B. C. Now the founding of Kirjath-sepher and the destruction of the Cities of the Plain have been shown to have been of that same period, hence the beginning of the nineteenth century B. C. Here for the first time appears a historical parallel at nearly 2,000 B. C. for the tragic event at Sodom. In our "Explorations at Sodom" we have estimated that catastrophe to have been early in the eighteenth century B. C. It now appears that it was a century earlier. This agrees well with the general consensus of opinion of Assyriologists now, that the call of Abram was near the end of the twentieth century or the beginning of the nineteenth B. C.

PARALLEL 4.—*The Twelfth and Thirteenth Dynasties of Egypt—and the Story of Abraham and Lot.* This now only needs to be stated; the evidence has already been adduced. Perhaps this is as near an exact date for that narrative and of the events there narrated, as we shall ever obtain.

PARALLEL 5.—*Abraham and Lot—and the Estimated Time of the Exodus.* The material for estimating the time from the call of Abram to the Exodus is not very extensive in the Bible. Biblical writers, not living in an age that estimated by our calendar, did not, as a matter of course, follow our method, and it is not easy to translate their data into our dates. There is rather general agreement that the Biblical data call for about 645 years between these two events. Now, if the Iron Age in Palestine began about 1200 B. C. and the taking of Kirjath-sepher in the Conquest soon after, then the Exodus would be about fifty years earlier (forty in the wilderness and ten in the Conquest); this would well agree with the call of Abram early in the nineteenth century. While these dates, being estimated and not stated in the Bible, are not perfectly exact and one may not pin his faith to them as though they were a revelation, yet they do afford an interesting and helpful parallel between independent lines of evidence.

PARALLEL 6.—*Social and Political Conditions at Sodom and at Gibeah—and the Conditions Evidenced by the Great Court of the End of Early Bronze Age and the Beginning of Middle Bronze at Kirjath-sepher.* The story of Lot and the men, really angels, come from Abraham to warn him, reveals social and political conditions in the doomed city. The angels proposed to remain in the street for the night. Lot would not hear of it; he well knew the men of Sodom and insisted that these strangers should accept the hospitality of his house for protection. Evidently also police protection was not to be relied upon at Sodom. The angels accepted Lot's invitation and the mob also accepted the temptation put before them and battered at the door. That was mob-proof; they did not get in. Exactly the same social and political conditions are revealed in the horrible tragedy at Gibeah of Benjamin. Such social and political conditions call for peculiar house construction. Not all houses are mob-proof. Now at Kirjath-sepher in the transition between Early and Middle Bronze, parallel, as we have seen, with the story of Lot, we found a great court of a house, probably a caravansary, that exactly fulfills these conditions, and was named at once by the staff, "The Abrahamic House." It had great walls, inside of which were conveniences for man and beast, and the great heavy door was made known by the great eight inch door socket still *in situ*. Such mob-proof doors are common in that age and also later in the Early Iron I, the time of the tragedy at Gibeah. The story in each case is in keeping with the conditions. The significance of all this becomes apparent only by contrast with the houses of the eighth and seventh centuries, at which time much critical acumen would have us believe the Biblical stories of Genesis were composed. The city of that time is here the best preserved of all the cities on the *tell*. A multitude of houses and scores of doors are now known. Door sockets of *any* size are all but unknown at that age. Social and political conditions permitted arches or curtains, certainly not mob-proof. Now how could the Lot narrative be produced in such an age and under such conditions? Was the writer a distinguished archæologist, who in the eighth century could reproduce the conditions of the nineteenth century? Verily the less faith people have the more they need in order to believe their own theories!

PARALLEL 7.—*The "Pest" in Egypt—and the Turmoil in the Middle Bronze Age at Kirjath-sepher.* The Hyksos were so hated in Egypt that the Egyptians never give us their ethnic name, but call them by opprobrious epithets among which is the "pest." In the Joseph story this is translated "abomination." So it is said, "Every shepherd is an abomination unto the Egyptians." These foreign rulers seemed to be against every one except the Israelites, who were accorded royal favor. It is interesting to note here the dreadful turmoil in Palestine in that age. Six cities of the Middle Bronze Age and the transition from the Early Bronze Age were built and destroyed here in three hundred to four hundred years.

PARALLEL 8.—*The "Sea Peoples" in Egyptian Literature— and in Palestinian Culture.* Nothing could be more striking than the change wrought in the pottery in this land by the change from the Middle Bronze Age to the Late Bronze Age. At this time pottery was imported from Cyprus and the Greek coast and then imitated in Palestine until at last we have the strange style known as Philistine with such garish decoration.

PARALLEL 9.—*The Philistine Culture—and the Desert Life of Israel.* That the Israelites were artists and craftsmen when they left Egypt is sure; that they lost these arts and crafts in the wilderness is equally certain. How could they do otherwise, when the old men died and the young men had no opportunity to learn in their simple desert life? This is exactly paralleled in the squatter settlement at Kirjath-sepher and the imitation of Philistine pottery.

PARALLEL 10.—*The Exodus at the Beginning of the Iron Age—and the Scarabs at Kirjath-sepher.* The Amenophis III scarab in the Late Bronze Age attests the presence of an Egyptian official at that time, and the imitation of a Nineteenth Dynasty Rameses scarab in Early Iron I indicates that Israelites were at *that* time in possession. In each case this is in harmony with the late date of the Exodus and out of harmony with the early date. And the great burned level at Kirjath-sepher exactly separates Canaanites and Israelites—the Late Bronze Age and Early Iron I.

PARALLEL 11.—*Jeroboam and Shishak—and the Destruction Wrought at Kirjath-sepher by Shishak.* The familiar Biblical account of Jeroboam's contest for the throne, and the coming of Shishak from Egypt to devastate both Northern and Southern Kingdoms is fully corroborated in the terrible burning of the city of the time of the Monarchy exactly coinciding with the time of Shishak.

Jeroboam had been a refugee in Egypt, whence he came back to contest for the throne of Solomon at that monarch's death. That Egypt would be on the *qui vive* politically was most in keeping with the intrigue of the nations of that age —and all other ages, for that matter—and that Jeroboam expected help from Shishak is to be understood as a matter of course, though not distinctly stated in the record. That Shishak "helped himself" is equally attested by the list of conquered cities in both kingdoms left by Shishak at Karnak.

PARALLEL 12.—*The Diatribe of Isaiah Against the Women of His Time for Their Vain Fashions—and the Vanity Cases Discovered at Kirjath-sepher.* He ridicules the women for their mincing walk and their elaborate hair-dressing and their rouge and lip-sticks. They had different names for these things in those days, but the fashions most remarkably resembled the extremes of fashionable "make-up" in these days. Scarcely a day went by when we were excavating the city of the kings of Judah that we did not find a vanity palette of one of those pampered ladies. It seems as if every Jewess in the town had one.

PARALLEL 13.—*Jehoiachin Jar Handles—and the Destruction by Nebuchadnezzar as Recorded in the Bible, of Whom It Is Said He "Destroyed the Fenced Cities of Judah."* The names of those cities are not given. Was Kirjath-sepher one of those destroyed? That the city was destroyed and left without rebuilding is easily apparent upon the most cursory examination; but who destroyed it? Zedekiah was king at the time of the actual capture of Jerusalem and nominally so at the final destruction of the cities of the land. Of him we have no definite record at Kirjath-sepher; but Jehoiachin reigned immediately before Zedekiah. His reign was the brief one of only three months and eight days. During the latter part of the period of the kings of Judah, from about the time of Hezekiah onward, there was in vogue the custom of using stamped jar handles upon a standard government jar for the reception of taxes paid in kind. Possibly an impression of the stamp was given to the tax-payer, which he retained as a kind of "finger-print" evidence which he could exhibit when called upon. Now we have found at Kirjath-sepher two jar handles with a stamp beautifully engraved, "To Eliakim the official servant of Jochin (the abbreviated Hebrew form of Jehoiachin)." A third of these jar handles was found by Dr. Grant at Beth-shemesh. Here, then, is documentary evidence, dated in a short reign of three months and eight days, which shows tax receipts being issued in the name of Jehoiachin immediately before the reign of Zedekiah and thus a short time before the destruction of the city by Nebuchadnezzar. It thus becomes certain that Nebuchadnezzar, and not Sennacherib or any other enemy at an earlier time, finally destroyed Kirjath-sepher.

PARALLEL 14.—*The Culture of the Various Ages—and the Culture Reflected in the Narratives Attributed to those Ages.*

The most important of the parallels developed here at Kirjath-sepher and illustrated throughout the land is the evidence supplied by the culture of the various ages compared with the culture reflected in the narratives attributed to those ages. This is indeed a comprehensive summing up of the evidence to sustain the theme of this book: The Culture of Bible Lands, the Matrix of Bible Narratives.

The earliest narratives of Abram reflect the culture of a primitive age. They are not lacking in literary character, but there is a quaintness in the customs of the people and a quality in the literary expression which reflects a quaintness, not a highly sophisticated life or artificial culture. The pottery of the time displays the same primitive character. It is usually rough, coarse and largely hand made, but strong and durable. Yet good things were made in that age. That one tall shapely pot, unmistakably Early Bronze in pattern and provenance, was found at Kirjath-sepher. It was of fine, thin ware and of attractive shape and finish. And from tombs in the Jordan Valley has come some beautiful distinctively Early Bronze ware. The comparison between the material remains and the narratives of this age are not so striking as in subsequent ages, and yet they are satisfying.

The narratives from the Patriarchal times of the Middle Bronze Age, 2000-1600 B. C., reflect intelligence and high culture; they did not come from ignorant people nor were they directed to ignoramuses. The critical theory to meet these representations is that the narratives do not come from the time of the events narrated, but from a time long subsequent, about the time of Hezekiah, a little before or a little after. Thus the appearance of culture in the literature belongs not to 2000-1600 B. C., but to about the eighth century B. C. Examination of Middle Bronze Age material reveals, however, an astonishingly high culture. The castle palaces of the feudal barons of that age, the exquisite pottery shapes which have been standard ever since and never improved upon, the beautiful alabstron bric-a-brac, and above all, the unsurpassed engraving of the seal cylinder show that age to have been indeed a time of the highest culture Palestine ever knew until Greek and Roman times, a culture which literature from the eighth century B. C. could not reflect.

The Late Bronze Age, 1600-1200 B. C., or a little later, is a time concerning which there are strange indications in literature. The *Tell el-Amarna* tablets tell of insurrections and invasions and general turmoil in the Palestinian province of Egypt. The Bible indicates in a graphic way the same state of affairs in the peculiar title given the land of Promise, "the place of the Canaanites, and the Hittites, and the Amorites, and the Perizzites, and the Hivites, and the Jebusites," certainly the descriptive title of a land which had no central government. The Egyptian records also tell of the "Sea-peoples" who came into Palestine at this time from Cyprus and the Greek Islands. Exactly in accord with these representations the pottery of this age is Cypro-Phœnician and Mycenæan in Palestine. The beautiful indigenous pottery of the Middle Bronze Age gives way completely to these imported styles. When people import all their best things, it is certainly a time of deterioration.

The next age, Early Iron I, saw the rise of the common people and the beginning of a new indigenous culture. The Israelites, highly skilled when they left Egypt, came into the Land of Promise two generations later having lost their arts and crafts in the simple wilderness life. Taught religion and statecraft, they were now an unskilled people. The material remains at Kirjath-sepher and everywhere in the land show exactly the same state of culture; their first building was of the crudest sort and their early pottery the simple pottery needed in the tent life of the wilderness. As they began to develop they learned from the Philistines, the descendants of the "Sea-people."

Early Iron Age II, the time of the kings of Judah, 900-600 B. C., never even in the palmiest days of the Israelite culture rose to the heights of the culture of the Patriarchal times. Instead, we find now a great industrial development, the greatest in the history of the land up to that time. The elaborate civil organization also of the Solomonic regime was perpetuated in both northern and southern kingdoms. Thus in every age the material remains show the same culture reflected in the literature attributed to that age.

The parallel in literature is often used to prove plagiarism and is denominated the "deadly parallel." These historical parallels that we have been considering are not "deadly," but specifically life-giving. Every recorded historical event claiming thus to be historical which is paralleled by another historical event of entirely independent record is thus certified as a real event, and when, as in all these cases, the evidence of the parallel event is material evidence dug up out of the ground, the attestation becomes unequivocal, may we not say indisputable. False records, even folk-lore and legends, represent events that are only imaginary; *and do not leave anything to be dug up out of the ground.*

We have been living and working and walking and talking in the land of the Book; we have noted its associations from the earliest times to the present. Thus have we seen its culture in all ages and have seen the Book among its friends and neighbors and enemies in ancient times and now. We have traced the footsteps of the Patriarchs down the Jordan Valley to the Great Break in civilization at the destruction of the Cities of the Plain; we have walked through the deprivations of the wilderness journey and followed the footsteps of the invading host as they entered the land for the Conquest, and have dug out the whole fossilized history of the end of the Conquest in the destruction of the last great guardian fortress of the south, Kirjath-sepher; and we have watched the development of the city into the industrial center of the days of the kings of Judah and its final destruction by Nebuchadnezzar. By actual experience and observation year after year we have learned the customs of the land and of the day as the customs of the Book, that, in fact, archæological history in Bible Lands is very like current events antedated.

Thus we have held sedulously to the theme from which we set out, the theme set on the title page, "The Culture of Bible Lands, the Matrix of Bible Narratives." Everywhere we have found the last and conclusive test of every life story; *the narrative fits the matrix.*

AMERICA AND THE HOLY LAND

An Arno Press Collection

Adler, Cyrus and Aaron M. Margalith. **With Firmness in the Right:** American Diplomatic Action Affecting Jews, 1840-1945. 1946

Babcock, Maltbie Davenport. **Letters From Egypt and Palestine.** 1902

Badt-Strauss, Bertha. **White Fire:** The Life and Works of Jessie Sampter. 1956

Barclay, J[ames] T[urner]. **The City of the Great King.** 1858

Baron, Salo W. and Jeanette M. Baron. **Palestinian Messengers in America,** 1849-79. 1943

Bartlett, S[amuel] C[olcord]. **From Egypt to Palestine.** 1879

Bliss, Frederick Jones. **The Development of Palestine Exploration.** 1907

Bond, Alvan. **Memoir of the Rev. Pliny Fisk, A. M.:** Late Missionary to Palestine. 1828

Browne, J[ohn] Ross. **Yusef:** Or the Journey of the Frangi. 1853

Burnet, D[avid] S[taats], compiler. **The Jerusalem Mission:** Under the Direction of the American Christian Missionary Society. 1853

Call to America to Build Zion. 1977

Christian Protagonists for Jewish Restoration. 1977

Cox, Samuel S. **Orient Sunbeams:** Or, From the Porte to the Pyramids, By Way of Palestine. 1882

Cresson, Warder. **The Key of David.** 1852

Crossman, Richard. **Palestine Mission: A Personal Record.** 1947

Davis, Moshe, editor. **Israel:** Its Role in Civilization. 1956

De Hass, Frank S. **Buried Cities Recovered:** Or, Explorations in Bible Lands. 1883

[Even, Charles]. **The Lost Tribes of Israel:** Or, The First of the Red Men. 1861

Field, Frank McCoy. **Where Jesus Walked:** Through the Holy Land with the Master. 1951

Fink, Reuben, editor. **America and Palestine:** The Attitude of Official America and of the American People. 1944

Fosdick, Harry Emerson. **A Pilgrimage to Palestine.** 1927

Fulton, John. **The Beautiful Land:** Palestine, Historical, Geographical and Pictorial.　1891

Gilmore, Albert Field. **East and West of Jordan.**　1929

Gordon, Benjamin L[ee]. **New Judea:** Jewish Life in Modern Palestine and Egypt.　1919

Holmes, John Haynes. **Palestine To-Day and To-Morrow:** A Gentile's Survey of Zionism.　1929

Holy Land Missions and Missionaries.　1977

[Hoofien, Sigfried]. **Report of Mr. S. Hoofien to the Joint Distribution Committee of the American Funds for Jewish War Sufferers.**　1918

Intercollegiate Zionist Association of America. **Kadimah.**　1918

Isaacs, Samuel Hillel. **The True Boundaries of the Holy Land.**　1917

Israel, J[ohn] and H[enry] Lundt. **Journal of a Cruize in the U. S. Ship Delaware 74 in the Mediterranean in the Years 1833 & 34.** 1835

Johnson, Sarah Barclay. **Hadji in Syria:** Or, Three Years in Jerusalem. 1858

Kallen, Horace M[eyer]. **Frontiers of Hope.**　1929

Krimsky, Jos[eph]. **Pilgrimage & Service.**　1918-1919

Kyle, Melvin Grove. **Excavating Kirjath-Sepher's Ten Cities.**　1934

Kyle, Melvin Grove. **Explorations at Sodom:** The Story of Ancient Sodom in the Light of Modern Research.　1928

Lipsky, Louis. **Thirty Years of American Zionism.**　1927

Lynch, W[illiam] F[rancis]. **Narrative of the United States' Expedition to the River Jordan and the Dead Sea.**　1849

Macalister, R[obert] A[lexander] S[tewart]. **A Century of Excavation in Palestine.**　[1925]

McCrackan, W[illiam] D[enison]. **The New Palestine.**　1922

Merrill, Selah. **Ancient Jerusalem.**　1908

Meyer, Isidore S., editor. **Early History of Zionism in America.**　1958

Miller, Ellen Clare. **Eastern Sketches:** Notes of Scenery, Schools, and Tent Life in Syria and Palestine.　1871

[Minor, Clorinda]. **Meshullam!** Or, Tidings From Jerusalem.　1851

Morris, Robert. **Freemasonry in the Holy Land.**　1872

Morton, Daniel O[liver] . **Memoir of Rev. Levi Parsons, Late Missionary to Palestine.** 1824

Odenheimer, W[illiam] H. **Jerusalem and its Vicinity.** 1855

Olin, Stephen. **Travels in Egypt, Arabia Petraea, and the Holy Land.** 1843. Two Vols. in One

Palmer, E[dward] H[enry] . **The Desert of the Exodus.** 1871. Two Vols. in One

Paton, Lewis Bayles. **Jerusalem in Bible Times.** 1908

Pioneer Settlement in the Twenties. 1977

Prime, William C[ooper] . **Tent Life in the Holy Land.** 1857

Rifkind, Simon H., et al. **The Basic Equities of the Palestine Problem.** 1947

Rix, Herbert. **Tent and Testament:** A Camping Tour in Palestine with Some Notes on Scriptural Sites. 1907

Robinson, Edward. **Biblical Researches in Palestine, Mount Sinai and Arabia Petraea.** 1841. Three Volumes

Robinson, Edward. **Later Biblical Researches in Palestine and in Adjacent Regions.** 1856

Schaff, Philip. **Through Bible Lands:** Notes on Travel in Egypt, the Desert, and Palestine. [1878]

Smith, Ethan. **View of the Hebrews.** 1823

Smith, George A[lbert] , et al. **Correspondence of Palestine Tourists.** 1875

Smith, Henry B[oynton] and Roswell D. Hitchcock. **The Life, Writings and Character of Edward Robinson.** 1863

Sneersohn, H[aym] Z[vee] . **Palestine and Roumania.** 1872

Szold, Henrietta. **Recent Jewish Progress in Palestine.** 1915

Talmage, T[homas] de Witt. **Talmage on Palestine:** A Series of Sermons. 1890

Taylor, Bayard. **The Lands of the Saracen:** Or, Pictures of Palestine, Asia Minor, Sicily, and Spain. 1855

The American Republic and Ancient Israel. 1977

Thompson, George, et al. **A View of the Holy Land.** 1850

Van Dyke, Henry. **Out-of-Doors in the Holy Land:** Impressions of Travel in Body and Spirit. 1908

Vester, Bertha [Hedges] Spafford. **Our Jerusalem:** An American Family in the Holy City, 1881-1949.   1950

Wallace, Edwin Sherman. **Jerusalem the Holy.**   1898

[Ware, William] . **Julian:** Or Scenes in Judea.   1841. Two Vols. in One

Worsley, Israel. **A View of the American Indians:** Showing Them to Be the Descendants of the Ten Tribes of Israel.   1828

Yehoash [Bloomgarden, Solomon] . **The Feet of the Messenger.**   1923